The **Purpose** *and*

Call of God

For Your Life

The Purpose and Call of God

For Your Life

Aldo John Hope

EPOH Publishers

Ordering Information:
Quantity sales: For details, contact the publisher at epohsales@gmail.com

The Purpose and Call of God for your Life

ISBN   978-9970-94550-4 (Paperback)
ISBN   978-9970-94900-7 (eBook)

Category - Christian Living/ Personal Growth, Spiritual Growth, Inspiration, Charismatic

First Edition, Cover, Layout & Formatting by Royal Exprexionz, royalexprexionz@gmail.com

Table of Contents

Acknowledgments

I am eternally grateful for the grace and inspiration of the Holy Spirit that enabled the compilation of this book. I further, wish to thank all those that supported me with prayers during the writing of this book.

Further, I particularly, thank those who dedicated their time to review and suggest improvements to the draft. I am grateful for the help received from the following persons; Bosco O., Patrick K. (Rev Fr.), Samuel M. (PhD), Vivian O., Dorcas N., Diana M B., Tansila N., Mark Douglas W. (PhD), Barbara N., Raphael W (Rev Fr.), John Baptist D (Rev Fr.), Augustine M., Godwin A., Dennis O., Rachael O.and my spouse Grace Hope. I sincerely thank Godwin A. and Robert Grace Kisenyi for their technical support.

I acknowledge and thank all whose names are not mentioned but who nevertheless supported the writing of this book. I further thank all those who taught and mentored me in the art and specifics of book writing.

Finally, I am grateful to all the members of my family who supported me in various ways. I am grateful to my parents and my sister Elizabeth N.J. I thank all my other sisters for their various support including distribution, channel, and sales (Florence A., Pyerina A.) and those who supported the publication of the book, (Tansila N., and Seraphine A.). I also thank all the little children; Michelle, Anne, Daniel and Ian for their patience.

I pray and hope that this book blesses and transforms the lives of those that prayerfully use it.

Introduction

We constantly wonder why one Christian is more victorious in their everyday assignments and life than ourselves and the Christian next door. We wonder why not all Christians are equally blessed, why some face strife, failure, poverty, lack, and similar misfortunes. We ponder this and often fail to get the right answer. We often propose several explanations and conclusions. When we take a keen look, we conclude that we are less blessed despite our commitment to our Christian life and walk. A casual spectator often notices that despite our sincere commitment to our Christian lives, we do not have it all together.

What could be the problem? Are we not all children of the same God, as the scriptures say, *"He causes his sun to rise on the evil and the good, and sends rain on the righteous and the unrighteous?"* (Matthew 5:45). Further, the Scriptures tell us that the Lord delights in our well-being. As captured in the book of Psalms; He is, *"The LORD, who delights in the well-being of his servant"* (Psalm 35:27) and promised to bless all the works of our hands (Deuteronomy 28:8,12).

We thus understand that the problem lies not with God. God is not to blame. He has set everything ready, for whosoever obeys, as scripture repeatedly reminds us. God loves us His children dearly. Everything is calm and peaceful in heaven. We can say that our requests are not being honored, and sadly, in a store or warehouse of God that is full of free gifts ready to be dished out. We are not able to receive from God as those other folks. Something is blocking us from receiving what God is more than willing to give us.

This question is easily answered when we honestly ask and answer the question, "What did God create me to do on earth, what did God send me to do on earth, why am I here on earth, and am I doing it?" We learn a very important truth in the book of Psalms. Psalm 139:13-18, declares that God created each one of us for a specific purpose and assignment on earth. He weaved us carefully, fearfully, wonderfully, and knew and determined ahead of time, all the days of our lives on earth. This was not for fun, but to help us live a fulfilled and victorious life.

The Lexico, Collins dictionary and others define "purpose" (noun) as; *"The reason for which something is done or created or for which something exists."* For this short period of our time on earth, we are expected to be actively engaged in doing God's purpose for our lives. The Lord knew and declared beforehand our end from the beginning, and his firm purpose for each of us, as the prophet Isaiah tells us, *"I make known the end from the beginning, from ancient times, what is still to come. I say, 'My purpose will stand, and*

I will do all that I please'" (Isaiah 46:10). This purpose and assignment was determined by God before our conception, and does not change (Romans 11:29). Scripture tells us that, *"Whoever does the will of God lives forever"* (1 John 2:17), while the book of Deuteronomy chapter 28 urges us to diligently obey the word of God and His commands, in order for the Lord to bless all the works of our hands (verse 12). Note that the Lord promises to bless not just one or two works of our hands, but all the works of our hands.

Why are all the works of our hands not blessed? In several areas, we Christians have been obedient to God in all sincerity- except in this one area, that is, God's purpose for our lives. This area remained veiled from us. Thus, we did not seek, know or do the purpose that God created us for. How can we do God's purpose for our lives when we do not know the exact purpose the Lord created us for? In other words, how can we know or figure out what the Lord created us for? What does a person need to do to know what the Lord God created them for, so as to begin to act on it? Knowing our life's purpose, that is, what God created us for, and doing it, enables us to avert failure.

Yet, due to peer pressure, we may be engaged in what the world fancies or esteems. In most instances, we are presently engaged in what the pressures and cares of life forced upon us, and not necessarily what the Lord created us for.

When we operate outside the purpose of God we labour in vain. The book of Psalms helps us to understand the importance of cooperating with God in the purpose He created us for. We are helped to understand why our works are most times not blessed, because they are not in the purpose of God. The Psalmist says, *"Unless the LORD builds the house, the builders labor in vain. Unless the LORD watches over the city, the guards stand watch in vain. In vain you rise early and stay up late, toiling for food to eat"* (Psalm 127:1-2).

What would you do if the Lord God showed you a way out of this predicament? What if God made it clear to you that He is with you to help you achieve this purpose, and all you have to do is to cooperate with Him? And that as a result, you overcome all unnecessary mishaps, challenges, misfortunes, failures, poverty that currently troubles you? This is definitely good news. This promise is not made up but is exactly what God promised, and the Lord Jesus too declared them. As stated in Paul letter to the Corinthians, *"no matter how many promises God has made, they are "Yes" in Christ"* (2 Corinthians 1:20).

There exists all manner of afflictions out there that should not be ours, if only we knew what the Lord God created us for and accepted to diligently obey and do them. We would be miles ahead and more fulfilled, compared to where we are right now. Yet, the enemy has all along hindered us from getting access to and receiving this critical knowledge, insight, wisdom, and revelation.

What would you do if you found someone that helped and supported you to overcome the failures in your path? This would be heavenly. This book provides godly insight to avert such failures and mishaps, by seeking, finding and doing the purpose that God created us for. When we are not in the purpose the Lord created us for the door is wide open for the enemy to fool us unhindered. We believe that there are challenges and situations that the Lord Jesus promised us. These strengthen us and are godly. However, there are countless challenges that are not for the Christian, and we ought not to bear with them, and most result from being out of the purpose of God for our lives.

The purpose of God for us is sacred. We receive provision and protection as we do it. As in Psalms 91 we are sheltered from unnecessary storms. It is the place where we are sheltered from the snares of Satan. It is where the Most High (Elyon), El-Shaddai (God the Almighty) and (The Lord God) Yahweh watches over us. Scripture highlights this in the book of Psalms thus; *"Whoever dwells in the shelter of the Most High will rest in the shadow of the Almighty. I will say of the Lord, "He is my refuge and my fortress, my God, in whom I trust"* (Psalm 91:1-2). So the purpose of God for us is not only sacred but a sure weapon of victory. In this Psalm, the Lord promises to among other things save us from the snare of the fowler (Satan's traps, deception, trickery and all other evils) and from the deadly pestilence (plague, devastating sickness, and disease).

The Lord also promises to give us angelic help, protect and deliver us from trouble. We are also promised a long life (Psalm 90:10; 91:16). But these are possible when we live in the purpose of God for our lives. Our foremost enemy, Satan, is well aware that when we get hold of our purpose and do it, we will walk in victory. His goal is to hinder us from knowing what our purpose is, and fulfilling it.

The Lord does not give us a purpose He knows we cannot carry out. The Lord equips those He calls. He is with us when we obey. He does not forsake, nor leave us to do it in our own strength. Thus, the enemy will put up a spirited fight to see that we do not move towards the purpose God created us for. The enemy will fight our effort in this direction in the same way he fights any child of God who does the right thing. The enemy tries (if we allow any inch of ground unprotected) to keep us in bondage.

We should not lose this fight because the Lord Jesus has already won it on our behalf. We need to dig out the truth, knowledge, wisdom, and revelation about the purpose of God for us, and use these to overcome the circumstances that beset us.

When we live in this purpose we are able to quit those things that do not matter that we have spent decades engaged in with minimal impact on us and those around us. This book helps us understand that God created us for a specific purpose and assignment. Furthermore, the book encourages us to seek, find and carry out the purpose God created us for while we still have a chance.

Short of that, we will be like a plane that traveled off-course (with disregard to the compass or radar) or an athlete running a wrong race and on a wrong course. The apostle Paul tells us that we have a race ahead of us. He says; *"And let us run with perseverance the race marked out for us"* (Hebrews 12:1). While the book of Proverbs counsels us to be careful about being out of the purpose of God. It says; *"Many are the plans in a person's heart, but it is the Lord's purpose that prevails"* (Proverbs 19:21).

When we find this purpose and do it, we will find fulfillment, joy, and peace and make the desired progress that impacts those around us and glorify God. We often come up with personal plans and ideas but we ought to find out and let that of the Lord prevail. It is in the purpose of God for us that we reach and achieve all that the Lord created us for. With God and in the purpose the Lord created us for we can do "greater things than these" that the Lord Jesus promised us in John 14:12. Act now, read and apply this truth to enable you live a triumphant and fulfilled life.

Chapter 1

We Are On Earth For A Specific Purpose

There are Christians who live near us. There are some more in the farther neighborhoods. And there are others in various locations around the world. Only a few of these Christians have the promised multi fold graces and blessings of God flowing towards them. These few Christians seem to always flow in divine favor. These blessed and victorious Christians are extremely few and some estimate them at less than a fifth of the population.

Whereas these victorious ones face similar suffering, strife, struggles, and challenges, they seem to overcome them. They view these challenges as opportunities to thrive. They tend to have more tangible fruits than others. While for the majority their daily condition cannot be described as such.

We are aware that all Christians are promised suffering, trials, and tests that enable them to grow and mature. We do not deny that. We are not talking about these kinds of trials and tests. Rather we are concerned about the ones that pull us down and make us less than Christ promised us. The ones that hinder us from achieving sustained Christ-like fruitfulness and results. Their struggles, pain, and challenges seem to produce less than anyone would expect. A few others find themselves in and out of misfortunes. We also encounter Christians that have fallen into poverty, and others that struggle constantly with poverty, and are seeking some way out of it. How do we explain the rampant poverty around us? How do we explain the extra effort and the hard work people put in only to come out with little to show for it? We often wonder what could be wrong.

But most of all, we wish we had truthful knowledge and information to overcome such circumstances. Yet around us, there are no shortages of advice we have received and for which we are truly grateful; except that we applied these without achieving the desired results. Thus, it is time to seek God for a solution to these challenges.

We ought to aim for Godly victory

We ought to aim for victory, rather than success (that is to say worldly success) in all that we do. When we pursue and seek success (as the world views it), we fall short, as this will be short term.

The word success means the attainment or accomplishment of our personal visions, goals, aims, and ambitions. Success has another connotation which is not exactly good for any Christian, as it also means the pursuit and achievement of worldly wealth, status and fame. It thus includes the attainment of self-actualization or similar distinguished acclaim. When we pursue success, the emphasis is on "me", "myself", and "I", instead of the Lord, my God and the glory of God. Thus, we focus on achieving our version of success, with minimal eternal impact.

We ought to seek and achieve the victory the Lord has in store for us. Victory should be our goal and concern. The victory in the Bible can be termed as *sâkal.* This Hebrew word means a wise and prudent "good success" and prosperity achieved with the help of God and not simply success. We should aim at overcoming adversities, challenges and setbacks with the help of God. Thus, with the help of the Lord, we conquer and win.

We should triumph in all we do with the

support of God. This should be against all odds and difficulties. Thus, with the help of the Lord, we conquer and win. We have to go up against every failure, poverty, calamities, and misfortunes and win. We ought to be triumphant in our efforts. This can happen when we have the help of God on our side. This help and grace of God then determines all the outcomes in our favor. The victory in this posture cannot be attributed to us, but only to the one who made it possible, God.

Our positioning gives us victory

The Lord God has promised to give us victory when we seek, find and carry out the purpose that He created us for. We overcome most of the persistent misfortunes and failures that have no bearing with the will of God when we seek, find and do the purpose God created us for. True victory and triumph comes from God and lasts for eternity. This victory is only possible when we obey the Lord. This enables us to be blessed in return.

The Lord has promised to cater for our needs when we carry out His purpose (see Matthew 6:33). We shall not lack (Psalm 23:1). God is not against our well-being. And He expects us to receive graces and resources from Him to build His kingdom. His word tells us that, the resources and wealth received from Him are to confirm, fulfill and keep the covenant He swore to our forefathers (Deuteronomy 8:18). We are to use them as He directs us, and to enable us abound in good works, and this results in thanksgiving to God (2 Corinthians 9:11).

When we receive wealth from God, we have to remember that the resources and wealth belong to Him. We have to use it frugally in moderation, and not flaunt it. We are only stewards of it (see Psalm 50:10, Haggai 2:8). The word of God says that *"The earth is the Lord's, and everything in it, the world, and all who live in it"* (Psalm 24:1).

To receive wealth from God we have to ask Him to show us how - it may well be an idea, concept, vision, or creativity. This idea or creativity enables us to provide specific services (or products) of value to the people of God. As we put this idea into practice, and serve the people, the blessing of God flows through us. Since, they flow through us, there is a portion that remains for us. When we carry this out, we produce tangible results. The resources received from the Lord are truly a blessing. We ought not to make them an idol or "god" to us. They should always remain secondary to our primary assignment, to know and glorify God. We have to seek and rely on the wisdom of God to make this idea work (see Proverbs 3-4).

We are advised not to love wealth or let it

ensnare us. It is an ungodly belief to think it is evil to engage in business. It may be that God has designed you to be a businessperson and nothing else. You have to seek God about your purpose. It is not evil to engage in a godly business, and indeed many would not survive if businesses did not exist. It is written in the book of Psalms that God delights in the well-being of His children (Psalm 35:27). And as stewards of His grace and blessings, we have to use the proceeds from these to advance His kingdom.

Paul the apostle tells us that *"God is able to bless you abundantly, so that in all things at all times, having all that you need, you will abound in every good work. As it is written: "They have freely scattered their gifts to the poor; their righteousness endures forever." Now he who supplies seed to the sower and bread for food will also supply and increase your store of seed and will enlarge the harvest of your righteousness. You will be enriched in every way so that you can be generous on every occasion, and through us, your generosity will result in thanksgiving to God"* (1 Corinthians 9: 8-10).

We are to use the resources and wealth that we receive from the Lord for various uses; for seed, bread for food, gifts to the poor, and other commitments. He desires that we lend and not borrow. We are called to be the head and not the tail, above and not underneath (see Deuteronomy

28:1-14). What we want to make sure is that we are involved in only the godly business the Lord has purposed for us. And stay clear of greed and unethical ways.

Gaius, David, Joseph, Abraham, Barnabas, and many others had sizeable wealth that they used to support the work of God. David gave all his wealth to build the temple (see 1 Chronicles 29:1-5). His wealth did not ensnare him. Barnabas sold his land and gave the proceeds to the church. What then is wrong with the accumulation of worldly wealth and focus on riches?

The Lord Jesus taught us not to focus, love or adore the accumulation of worldly wealth and riches, even when we have it, or because, indeed we all have some of it. We are to focus on the Lord Jesus and not on wealth. The poor likewise may become ensnared and guard or focus on the little they have. Alternatively, they too may worry unnecessarily about the need to accumulate wealth by some ungodly means.

Scriptures teach us to focus on Christ *"fixing our eyes on Jesus, the pioneer, and perfecter of faith. For the joy set before him, he endured the cross, scorning its shame, and sat down at the right hand of the throne of God"* (Hebrews 12:2). We would focus on such wealth to our peril, as scripture says; *"For where your treasure is, there your heart will be also"* (Matthew 6:21).

The Lord Jesus taught us to focus on genuine riches, and thus open to receive all riches; *"Do not store up for yourselves treasures on earth, where moths and vermin destroy, and where thieves break in and steal. But store up for yourselves treasures in heaven, where moths and vermin do not destroy, and where thieves do not break in and steal"* (Matthew 6:19-20).

Paul teaches us in 1 Timothy 1:6-10; that the love of money is a root of all kinds of evil, and that godliness with contentment is great gain. We should be content with what the Lord has blessed us with. The Lord Jesus cautioned us against focusing on wealth, saying that mammon chokes the word of God and makes it not bear fruit. As written in Mark 4:19; *"but the worries of this life, the deceitfulness of wealth and the desires for other things come in and choke the word, making it unfruitful."*

What are we to do then? We are promised provision and the true wealth that comes from God when we obey God and do His purpose. The wealth that does not come from God may be harmful as many scriptures help us know. The Lord told the rich young ruler to sell his possessions and give to the poor, and then come follow Jesus. He would then be rewarded multiple times with true wealth. The wealth received from God as He leads us is a blessed wealth that we use for ourselves and to support and advance His work (see Proverbs 10:22).

God promised to give us the ability to make wealth and so fulfill, confirm, keep the covenant He swore to our forefathers, and enable us flow and abound in good works and generosity that results in thanksgiving to God.

The Lord promises us in Matthew 6:33; *"But seek first his kingdom and his righteousness, and all these things will be given to you as well."* We are told not to focus on wealth, but to seek, and serve God, and we will be provided for. Such wealth received from the Lord should be used with joy, in the direction the Lord is pleased with, as faithful stewards, to bless God, ourselves and others. As stewards, we have to be frugal, live within our means, avoid debt as far as we can, save and invest as the ants do (Proverbs 6: 6-8).

The world's success contrasts sharply with the victory the Lord gives to those involved in building His kingdom. There are a fair number of those that have achieved (often by the grace of God) what seems like a worldly success. A few have used the resources and wealth at their disposal to build the kingdom of God and the Lord has blessed them further. The others do not imagine that their wealth should ever be used to advance the kingdom of God. Yet, the Lord Jesus taught us in Luke 9:25; *"What good is it for someone to gain the whole world, and yet lose or for-*

feit their very self?" The Lord provides us a timely caution to help us avoid the snare of success attained without the grace of God.

We Are Called To Live A Fulfilled Life

We Christians should not believe that our lot in life is that of dire poverty, failure, and misfortunes. There are extremes to know of here. There are those that live in total lack and poverty, but unfortunately, believe that it is the will of God for them. These need the truth of God's word to liberate them from this ungodly belief. They need to know the nature, mind, character and heart of God our Father towards us His children, and what He purposed for us from the very beginning. While others in a similar state of poverty, do not believe that poverty is of God, and are currently seeking God and taking practical actions to overcome it.

These should be commended. In the mid-ground are those with wealth and means that they readily put to the service of God and the advance of His kingdom. They are not ensnared by their wealth. They too should be commended. While at the extreme are those ensnared by their wealth (of any value and quantity, and may even include the poor) and other resources at their disposal. These do not see any need for God. Others see the need of God, but no need to use the resources at their disposal to advance the kingdom of God.

We know that the Lord Jesus (and the Holy Scriptures) condemn the love of wealth, avarice and the preoccupation with storing up earthly treasures and riches (Matthew 6:19-24; 1 Timothy 6:10; Hebrews 13:5, Proverbs 28:10). So where should we be? There is a place for us to receive, what is ours as stated in this same passage of Matthew 6 (see verse 33). The place for us to receive the blessings that the Lord kept for us from the beginning of age is in the purpose the Lord created us for.

The wealth that the Lord blesses us with is a great blessing to many other people. In a sense, we all have some wealth, gifts, and material endowment. Wealth received from God is to be put to good use, and we all receive such on regular basis. Wealth's source, type, size and our hearts posture towards it, and how we use it is what counts (stewardship). It is most beneficial when we are not trapped, enslaved, or ensnared by any wealth and use it to bless God and His kingdom. This enables many people to benefit directly and indirectly, from what the Lord has entrusted to us.

Short term lack and denial is certainly beneficial. However, poverty (long term) is such a bad thing that no one should entertain it. To overcome poverty, we have to first seek God to show us why He created us (His purpose) and do it, and at the same time ask God to give us an idea, vision, concept, creativity, that we can pursue. We should not be afraid to ask the Lord to show us a practical undertaking that creates value to God's people and blesses them and ourselves and those around us. It is often closely related to our gifts and talents, and the purpose of God for our lives. Thus a Christian may be truly committed, but out of the purpose of God, and wonder why they cannot make ends meet.

James the brother of Christ tells us that, we have not because we ask not, or ask improperly; *"You desire but do not have, so you kill. You covet but you cannot get what you want, so you quarrel and fight. You do not have because you do not ask God. When you ask, you do not receive, because you ask with wrong motives, that you may spend what you get on your pleasures"* (James 4:2-3). Therein lies the secret, that in the purpose of God for our lives, the Lord Has promised provision.

It is true that the Lord Jesus promised that those who follow him will suffer for his sake. There are sufferings, trials and tests that the Lord has promised us Christians, but that cannot be long term failure, dire poverty and misfortunes of the type we cannot benefit spiritually from. The poverty of spirit in Matthew 5:3 means that we need to fill ourselves with more of God and help us desire to always seek God, but is not a direction to seek poverty.

We may have no access to jobs, but certainly, the Lord has much work for us to do (Luke 10:2). Satan should not pull away from us what is rightfully ours. The Lord has promised those laboring in the purpose of God for them to grant them this wish. He has promised many more returns to those who forsake their ambitions to follow him. He paid a huge price to enable us live in victory. *"Truly I tell you," Jesus replied, "no one who has left home or brothers or sisters or mother or father or children or fields for me and the gospel will fail to receive a hundred times as much in this present age: homes, brothers, sisters, mothers, children, and fields—along with persecutions—and in the age to come eternal life"* (Mark 10:29-30).

The Lord Jesus promised to take care of all our needs if and when we get involved in carrying out the purpose of God for our lives. The Lord becomes our personal source and provider, and He (the Lord) cannot fail (see Matthew 6:33, Psalm 89:34). This point is important because most people run away from God, the Church or the purpose of God for their lives citing the financial uncertainty that could be involved.

They shy away from seeking God and believe that they may starve to death if they get involved in carrying out the work of God. They bring to mind imaginations of some failed disciples, and how these struggled financially and lived below the dignity and glory of God. Yet all that happened was that such followers of God did not seek God wholeheartedly for an idea or vision or practical wisdom to this end. Such a disciple wrongly believed and concluded that serving God in the right purpose is possibly futile.

As Christians, we are followers of Christ, and seek to be Christ-like. The Lord Jesus did not suffer from lack. He was richly provided for. He had a finance director (in the name of Judas Iscariot), paid taxes and did not incur any known debt. He led a successful nationwide ministry, with a team of twelve apostles, many disciples and a vast crowd. He was born in a lowly place (a manger), due to travel challenges and to fulfill several prophecies and the will of God. Yet even at birth, He was richly provided with gold, frankincense and myrrh of some good value from high ranking wise men.

He sought not to flaunt His wealth. He fed thousands of people, at a short notice, proving that He had access to heavenly provision and source of immeasurable silver or gold value, at any point time. Twelve baskets, at the first count and seven at the subsequent count were left, and He ordered they should not be wasted. Some wealthy persons wholeheartedly supported Him. Read the accounts for yourself and you will agree that the Lord Jesus was not poor.

As God, He had means, and controlled all the cattle on a thousand hills, and gold and silver (Psalms 50:10, Haggai 2:8) but chose not to flaunt it. He ate well, dressed well, gave alms regularly, and had where to stay (home hospitality) where-ever He went. At the cross, He became poor in-order that we might be rich; *"For you know the grace of our Lord Jesus Christ, that though he was rich, yet for your sake he became poor, so that you through his poverty might become rich"* (2 Corinthians 8:9).

Anyone carrying out faithfully and diligently the purpose of God shall not be in want. The Lord is our personal provider and source, and provides in the most unusual ways. We should not bow down to the enemy to snatch from us what is rightfully ours as children of God. The Lord Jesus tells us in John 10:10 that, *"The thief comes only to steal and kill and destroy; I have come that they may have life, and have it to the full."* The Lord purchased this full and abundant life for us at the high cost of his own life. To achieve victory we have to forfeit our desires and plans and carry out the purpose the Lord created us for.

God Foreknew And Fore-Appointed Us

When the Lord created us, and before we were conceived or born, He already had a specific purpose and assignment for us on earth. He knew beforehand where and how we would co-labor with Him on earth. Psalm 139:13-18; captures the thoughts and mind of God about this;

> *For you created my inmost being; you knit me together in my mother's womb. I praise you because I am fearfully and wonderfully made; your works are wonderful, I know that full well. My frame was not hidden from you when I was made in the secret place when I was woven together in the depths of the earth. Your eyes saw my unformed body; all the days ordained for me were written in your book before one of them came to be* (Psalm 139:13-18).

The Lord knew and "saw" us before we were formed, and ordained (ordered, decreed, installed, inducted, appointed) our days beforehand. He knew and ordered our purpose beforehand. We have to take advantage of this truth. We have His favor and victory over us at its best, when we seek, find and do that which He created us for. Obedience to the purpose of God for us is the way out of the numerous mishaps facing us.

Those blessed folks living in the purpose of God for their lives have much to thank God for. We all realize how God's favor flows towards them. They do not need to look back, despite the challenges they may face. It is possible that their loved ones prayed and made intercession for them, and they readily found and accepted the purpose of God for their lives. This could, for example, be due to the gracious prayer of their grannies, aunties, uncles, mum, dad, or the intercession of faithful saints of God. In this way, most Christians have unknowingly and without hindrance entered into the purpose and plan of God for their lives.

Find Your Purpose

It is important to dig deep and find out the reason for our existence. We may have some knowledge and insight to start with, or we may not. We can also agree that if our past methods, efforts, and occupations did not achieve much, there must be a better way. We have the truth of God's word and the Holy Spirit living inside of us to help us and show us the purpose the Lord sent us to accomplish on earth.

We ought to persevere in this search, no matter how long it takes us. We are not able to carry out the purpose of God for our lives unless we initially find out what exactly it is. This search requires us to read, meditate and ponder the word of God, over and over, till everything falls in line. When we find our purpose, we should re-orient our entire life towards this one divine call. Our reason for existence is what should consume us and energize us.

When we do not find, accept and do the purpose the Lord created us for, we can only expect failure and lack of peace. This is something that we ought to avoid at all costs, especially once we discover our purpose. When we obey the purpose of God for our lives, the Lord provides for us, and protect us. The purpose that the Lord has chosen for us is where we rule and reign. We have access to heavenly resources to help us thrive in the purpose, and assignment of God for our lives.

God our loving Father is more than interested to reveal to us the purpose He created us for. Father God has a vast ripe field that requires many laborers, than is currently available. And there are no failures, poverty, or misfortunes in heaven much less in any of God's kingdom on earth. And anyone involved in carrying out the purpose of God for their lives has access to heavenly provisions adequate to the task. It is only fair that the Lord provides the requirements to do His work.

There is no unemployment in the kingdom of God. The kingdom of God has a shortage of laborers. Anyone that has sought employment for such a long time (without finding one) ought to ponder this same discussion. We have our share (that awaits us) in advancing the kingdom.

The Wisdom Of God Is Superior

Most people including motivational speakers have supported us over the years. These people love us and have good thoughts about us. They urge us to find our passion, look inside, work hard, persevere, think clearly, follow our guts, follow this and that key or formulas and similar advice. They impart all these to us so that we would succeed. These speakers are to be commended for their boldness and clearheadedness. We ought to thank them for taking the road less traveled to help us accomplish something in life. Some of their advice enabled some folks to achieve some of the things they suggested.

For the majority of us, however, much of the motivational advice has not been fruitful. In other cases, the motivational advice yielded less than the desired results. We admit that there was some knowledge or wisdom we missed. There was a gap. We thus acknowledge that we require truth from the one that created us (that is God) to overcome these gaps and blocks in our path. We ought to value and apply the Lord's advice and counsel ahead of all other advice.

Seek The Lord For Answers

We sometimes experience hardships and unexplainable challenges. This may include job losses, financial mishaps, marriage challenges and similar ones too many to list. We realize that these challenges should ideally not have approached or reached our tent, camp or home. This is because we are convinced that we are committed Christians in every sense of the word. We should have been safe and far off from such. They seem odd and unexplainable. We sense that we are not where we are supposed to be. There may be other reasons for our mishap. It is time to find out if any negative circumstance in our homes or communities is due to disobedience to the purpose of God for our lives. Does the Lord want to get our attention to get back to His purpose and plan for us?

Our Age And Status Do Not Matter

Our loving Father has no respect for time and space. They all work to His favor. There is then no need for us to despair concerning our age. Do not say "I am too young". Neither should any grown-up say "I am too old". Age is an advantage when it comes to doing the mission and assignment God created us for.

The Holy Scriptures tell us that many entered the purpose of God for their lives at a ripe old age. While many more were called at a tender age. The great people in the Bible found their purposes at various ages of their lives. For example, Moses started to lead the children of Israel when he was eighty years old. The patriarch Abraham, David, Peter, Paul, John, and the Judges Othniel, Deborah, Gideon, Jephthah, Barak, and the others began their assignments at various ages. It is neither too late nor too early to begin to impact the kingdom.

Our level of education and level of intelligence may not matter to the Lord that much either. The apostle Peter and a few others were fishermen and were accepted that way by the Lord Jesus. They did not have to rely on their level of education. They were not highly educated. This truth sounds illogical for our modern world, yet remains true, and one can stretch and attain the required knowledge and education after committing to the purpose. The appropriate opportunity to get the training for your purpose will avail itself. The Lord is prepared for such.

The Lord Jesus told his disciples, *"When you are brought before synagogues, rulers and authorities, do not worry about how you will defend yourselves or what you will say, for the Holy Spirit will teach you at that time what you should say"* (Luke 12:11-12). The flip side is that when we have a higher level of education pride may creep in and make us shun the Lord. The Lord's work may appear demeaning. There is a place, for the young, old, educated and uneducated in the kingdom of God.

Your focus should be that there must be an important purpose and assignment God created you for. Do not focus on your status, poverty or wealth, or age or your level of education. And your priority and urgency is that you are not going to rest until you find the purpose of God for your life and begin to pursue it. Or if you are already in the purpose the Lord created you for, we encourage you to be steadfast.

You want to avoid running a wrong race on earth, which was not meant for you. Your desire is to please God and live victoriously. You have to look up to God for help. When you find this precious pearl, do not waste any further time, instead, begin to pursue it with all your heart.

Let Us Not Stand By And Watch

The Lord created and fashioned each one of us to be unique. We are meant to complement each other and not be a carbon copy. We know that some people have so fully embraced the purpose and call of God for their lives. They are so sold out that they seem to be fulfilling two or three purposes at any one time. They have discovered joy in doing this. This gives us hope that we too can seek, discover and accept the purpose of God for us. Why would someone joyfully complete two or three purposes of God while we who are equally called stand by and watch?

Chapter 2

Victory Is In The Purpose Of God

We are created to triumph. This means that we are to prevail against big and frightening circumstances and realities. When we live our lives without any resistance from Satan, we are possibly going in the same direction as him. For us to triumph, we have to rely on God (and cooperate with Him) to use us to do His work.

When we diligently carry out the purpose of God for our lives, we should expect obstacles, setbacks and hindrances. However, we overcome them with the help of God. The obstacles help us know if we are on the right path, as God solves them for us. When we are on the wrong path, there will be no help forthcoming. The best place for the Lord God to fight battles on our behalf is when we are actively pursuing His divine purpose for our lives.

We find several examples of such cases in the bible. For instance, Moses, Joshua, David, Gideon, Samuel, Jehoshaphat all attributed their victory to the Lord's help.

We also encounter Zerubabbel who was given the gigantic task of rebuilding the Jerusalem temple. Fortunately, he was to rely on the help of God. The Lord gave this assurance to Zerubbabel through the prophet Zechariah. The word of God given to him through the prophet strengthened and encouraged him. He was able to undertake the gigantic task of rebuilding the temple. Here is what the Lord God told Zerubbabel;

> *So he said to me, "This is the word of the Lord to Zerubbabel: 'Not by might nor by power, but by my Spirit,' says the Lord Almighty. "What are you, mighty mountain? Before Zerubbabel, you will become level ground. Then he will bring out the capstone to shouts of 'God bless it! God bless it!'" Then the word of the Lord came to me: "The hands of Zerubbabel have laid the foundation of this temple; his hands will also complete it. Then you will know that the Lord Almighty has sent me to you. "Who dares despise the day of small things, since the seven eyes of the Lord that range throughout the earth will rejoice when they see the chosen capstone in the hand of Zerubba-*

bel? (Zechariah 4:6-10).

He rebuilt the temple during a trying time. This was a post-Babylonian exile period. How on earth was Zerubbabel ever going to be able to re-build such a gigantic temple by himself? Fortunately, he received the word and the will of God to do it. He was to rely on God, and not on his own might or power.

He was to start from "small beginnings and not despise it", possibly starting with one brick or block. Therefore, when the Lord God has spoken and commissioned us to do anything, we have the assurance of victory. The Lord desires us to live and carry out the purpose He created us for. To do this we have to rely on His help as Zerubbabel did. We ought to start small and progress to fulfill His purpose for our lives. Whereas God created us to have dominion over the earth (Genesis 1:18), we lost this right due to the fall of Adam. Yet, it is comforting to know that the Lord Jesus has restored all that we lost due to the fall of Adam.

Paul in his letter to the Romans assures us that through the Lord Jesus we have received abundant provision of grace to live in victory. *"For if, by the trespass of the one man, death reigned through that one man, how much more will those who receive God's abundant provision of grace and of the gift of righteousness reign in life through the one man, Jesus Christ!"* (Romans 5:17).

The place where we have our victory is in the purpose of God for our lives. We rule and reign in this place due to the power and authority handed down to us by God to thrive in this area. It is the place where the Lord Jesus has promised us and given us a green light to do greater things, "than these".

What greater things can anyone do than the Lord Jesus did? It has to be only "those things" the Lord himself, allows us, empowers us and enables us to do as He so desires. It can be in magnitude or extent, for example, you cover more geographical areas, heal more deaf people, feed millions, reach more numerically, raise more dead people and many others. He works through us to achieve such.

We should not take the credit, as it is He who does it through us. We become His hands, feet, eyes, ears, mouth, and instrument to use. How else is the Lord to operate on earth? The answer is through us and by our cooperation. This can only happen when we obey and do the things He created us for; *"Very truly I tell you, whoever believes in me will do the works I have been doing, and they will do even greater things than these because I am going to the Father"* (John 14:12).

The Lord promised that we are to be the head and not the tail if we fully obey His commandments. The Word of God in Deuteronomy chapter 28 assures us of victory if we walk in the will of God, and failure if we do not. The ultimate obedience is following the purpose and call of God for us. We are promised several blessings in that chapter if we fully obey the will and commands of the Lord. *"All these blessings will come on you and accompany you if you obey the Lord your God"* (Deuteronomy 28:2).

The apostle Paul encourages us to live in the perfect will and purpose of God for similar reasons. Paul teaches us that by doing so, we shall bear much fruit. He says, *"We continually ask God to fill you with the knowledge of his will through all the wisdom and understanding that the Spirit gives, so that you may live a life worthy of the Lord and please him in every way: bearing fruit in every good work, growing in the knowledge of God"* (Colossians 1:9-10). Thus, according to this and many other Scriptures when we live in the perfect will and purpose of God we bear much fruit.

We will find it extremely difficult to "rule and reign" (that is to triumph and live in victory) when we choose to live outside of the purpose of God (that is the specific purpose of God for our lives). This is irrespective of whether we are doing this knowingly or unknowingly. We will have glimpses of victory, but, this won't last.

Most people compare living outside the purpose of God for our lives to an attempt to fit a square peg in a round hole. We may succeed in the sense of the world, but fail to find peace, joy, and fulfillment. This lack of peace and fulfillment should help us realize that something is missing. We will feel as if we are misfits, or even "trapped" in most assignments and missions we are in. We may fail to understand or explain the recurrent turmoil inside of us.

When we are outside of the purpose of God, our life and circumstances will be in continual unnecessary strife and struggle. Our progress and victory will be minimal. We will not progress as expected in the true spiritual sense. Our true emotional, physical or material progress is retarded. Those around us will notice this but offer no explanation. We will probably look forward to retirement or a transition from the current roles. We will look forward to unnecessary rest and recuperation from time to time. In the worst instances, we will seek assignments primarily for the material gains attached to them. That is only a glimpse of the restless state described in Deuteronomy 28.

Failure Awaits Us Outside The Purpose Of God

When we live outside the purpose of God, it will be difficult to make any meaningful progress, instead we will continually fall short. Junior persons will overtake us (become our seniors) wherever we are. This is not to say that it is a bad thing to hand over, or train a successor. We will know in our heart that it shouldn't have happened that way. These are early warning shots to let us know the heart of God in this matter.

The Lord allows such circumstances to help us seek His true path for our lives. One of the ways the Lord speaks to us is by such circumstances. We will be out of favor with most people, including debtors who either die or close shop in the most unusual way. These are signals from the Lord that we should be grateful for.

We have to be wary, where, when we provide support, we do not receive any appreciation. We ought to be more careful when we discover that this reoccurs as a pattern. Sometimes we will lose engagement or employment that the Lord knows is not suitable for us. We have to be grateful and seek only the ones he wants us to do. We have to start all over again.

Other times we may collaborate in partnership with others and conclude the assignments. Yet receive no payment. Alternatively, we are paid a pittance and the partners disappear with whatever is left of our payment. Frequently, the assignment itself fails with possible litigation. Such are warning signs. And we need to get to the bottom of the matter as to what the Lord is speaking to us. There is something the Lord would like us to hear and adhere to. These occurrences are not bad in themselves unless we miss what the Lord is telling us.

We ought to labor only where the favor of the almighty God heavily rests upon us. It cannot be that we were created by the loving Father and sent into the world to fail. There is no failure in heaven. And so on earth, as it is in heaven. The Lord has promised never to leave us, nor fail us, nor abandon us (see Deuteronomy 31:6, Hebrews 13:5). To fail would mean that either God failed us, or failed to help us, or failed to deal with our enemies. An ordinary parent would not allow his child to fail, and God is not about to fail us, because it is not His nature.

The Lord showed himself to Moses and revealed to him his nature. Scripture gives us a part of the nature of God in this passage of Exodus; *And he passed in front of Moses, proclaiming, "The Lord, the Lord, the compassionate and gracious God, slow to anger, abounding in love and faithfulness, maintaining love to thousands, and forgiving wickedness, rebellion, and sin"* (Exodus 34:6-7). We are on earth to triumph with the help of God against all odds. God uses us as His instruments for his designs.

When we face failures as a consistent pattern there is an urgent need to seek God to reveal the cause. This helps us to reach God for the solution. God is not a God of failure. Scripture tells us that the Lord is *"Able to do immeasur-*

ably more than all we ask or imagine, according to his power that is at work within us" (Ephesians 3:20). We need not be afraid to seek God about anything, even when it looks trivial. Thus, certain persistent setbacks and upsets, including failures, lack, financial insufficiencies, joblessness, and barrenness are not in the perfect will of God. They are not the nature of God. Fortunately, with the Lord, nothing shall be too hard to overcome. The Lord provided the perfect solution and remedy for all such calamities more than 2000 years ago in Christ Jesus.

Provisions Are In The Purpose Of God

When we live in the purpose the Lord created us for, Father God takes over the cares for our provisions and protection. This is not wishful thinking. It is written in blood. It has been paid for in blood. He has promised it, it is an agreement, a covenant, and a strong one. It is difficult to explain and convince someone about this point. The simplest example to give would be that of an employee, working for an excellent, genuine and wealthy employer.

When anyone works for such an organization, they do not worry about their pay or benefits at all. This point does not cross their mind. Such employees put in a lot of effort to excel in their job and climb the ladder. In the book of Deuteronomy 8:18, the Lord promised to provide wealth for us as a way of keeping, fulfilling and confirming the covenant that He swore to our forefathers. It is in his word, and his word never fails.

All our known and unknown needs; finances, food, clothing, education, shelter, protection, and health are upon Him. Not that they will drop from heaven, possibly not. Rather, He provides and reveals to us specific and certain ways to receive them, and as we cooperate and obey His instructions, they become available. There are ways He will show us to live and thrive. He may decide to give us a unique idea, or creativity, or a concept, a vision to put into practice to achieve this end. Alternately He may grant us a chain of benefactors. This enables us to provide products and services of value to people around us. This enables the graces and blessing of God to flow through us.

He may show us or involve us in a unique investment. We may attract persons that support what the Lord has put in our hearts to do and are currently involved in. It is all upon him. This is confirmed by the Lord in Matthew 6:33-34; *"But seek first his kingdom and his righteousness, and all these things will be given to you as well. Therefore, do not worry about tomorrow, for tomorrow will worry about itself. Each day has enough trouble of its own."*

Similarly, the Lord has decreed in Psalm

23:1 that He is our provider and source. He will never forsake the righteous nor allow their children to beg (Psalm 37:25). He will provide all our needs according to his glorious riches in Christ Jesus (Philippians 4:19). The Lord has millions of different ways to make this come to pass.

Purpose Overcomes Incessant Worry

When we begin to live in this truth, we are free of endless strife and worries. Whenever fear, worry, stress, and anxiety assail us, we are better able to confront them and overcome them with the help of God. We no longer agree with them, nor allow them to take root. This hope helps us overcome the worries, anxieties, and stress that creep in due to the circumstance around us.

Those that lived in the purpose of God for their lives (for example Moses, David, Peter, Paul, and many others) knew this truth and did not bend to fear, worry, anxiety and stress. They stood firm in the face of adversity. They sang praises and worshiped God with gratitude even while in jail. They were happy and joyful whether inside jails or out of it. They were not afraid to die. Those that imprisoned them could not understand them. When we hear and know that God has told us to do something the pressure lifts off of us.

When we determine to carry out our own purposes, we will face unnecessary pressure and anxiety, and these can be harmful to our health. Medical experts too caution us about excessive stress, worry and anxiety, and mention them as factors in the cause and increase of ill health and death. Since we know how blessed we are when we walk in obedience to the purpose and assignment the Lord has created us for, we need not tolerate them. It is said that more than 90% of the things we worry about never happen. Most of the things that worry us are temporary. The enemy uses fear, worry and anxiety to trap us, and make us become irrational in these states. When we worry it does not change the situation.

It is better to be concerned as much as we can rather than worry. The concern makes us seek a solution. Worry and concern (care) are not the same things. The concerned person does not panic in a situation, they remain calm and collected. They acknowledge the grace, ability, and might of God to solve and overcome any situation. They seek the help, grace, and wisdom of God in such a circumstance.

The panicky person immediately sees hopelessness in a situation. They realize that others have harmed them, and they figure out how to get even and strike back. They find at least one scapegoat to work with. They do not seek to find the spiritual cause of the problem. They seek revenge, court action, compensation and similar remedy. They do all these before seeking God's view and perspective in the matter. When all fails, it will be time for them to seek God. Later on, when everything calms down, they realize they should have used God's wisdom to overcome the situation.

Scripture warns us continually about worrying. This is because it is the opposite of faith. It is not a fruit of the Holy Spirit. It is a harmful negative meditation on the things we ought to act on with the courage and wisdom of God. It consumes and wrecks our immune system, helping to trigger uncalled for medical challenges. To solve such worry, fear and anxiety we ought to do the opposite. We should instead sing and shout praises, give unending thanks and glory to God.

King Jehoshaphat was required by God, to sing praises to God while en-route to a battlefield. And it worked in his favor. He was glad that he obeyed. We ought to replace these negative forces with faith, love, and hope, peace joy patience, perseverance, kindness, faithfulness, goodness, gentleness, and self-control - the fruits of the Holy Spirit. When we magnify God instead of the challenge, we diminish the challenge and face it with the help of God. In this way we easily overcome it.

Almost all harsh circumstances are temporary. When we reflect on them in years to come, they will look minuscule, distant and insignificant. We will wonder why we gave them so much inappropriate attention. The gratitude (thanksgiving) and praises from us magnifies and glorifies God, who in turn wipes out the challenge. We better ask God to reveal to us the heavenly significance of what is troubling us. What is the will of God in all this? What does He require us to do in these tough circumstances?

The Joy Of The Lord Is Our Strength

We are much more blessed to be in a state of gratitude. We should not live in a state of grief, grumbling, complaining and strife. Anytime such hits us, we have to get back on track. We have so many great things that the Lord has done for us. We have so much to thank God for. These makes us have hope and know that the Lord is able to keep us safe and see us through any challenge.

We do not have to harp on our current mishaps. The Lord has allowed these circumstances to beset us and shape us so that we look up to Him for the solutions. The Lord allows them, but He does not cause them *"For God is not a God of disorder but of peace"* (1 Corinthians 14:33). Our future is bright because we have placed our trust in Him; *"You will keep in perfect peace those whose minds are steadfast because they trust in you"* (Isaiah 26:3).

We ought to soar high above challenges by magnifying Him who is greater than the challenges. And He is able to keep us from falling and help us overcome all obstacles when we receive His wisdom. In the book of Nehemiah, the Israelites began to mourn and weep when the law was read to them. That day they recommitted themselves to the covenant of the Lord. Ezra read the entire law and this became an emotional moment for them. Nehemiah counseled them and told them to rejoice, and not weep for (he told them) the day was sacred in the eyes of the Lord. This is what he said to them;

> *Go and enjoy choice food and sweet drinks, and send some to those who have nothing prepared. This day is holy to our Lord. Do not grieve, for the joy of the Lord is your strength.* (Nehemiah 8:10).

When we obey God we are able to press into our victory no matter the circumstance. The circumstances work in our favor as happened for Joseph, Moses, David, the prophets and the apostles. We need joy and peace instead of fear, stress, worry, and anxiety.

We Learn From Failed Projects

Wherever we go we find many failed projects. This is sad as the owners put in a lot of time, toil, tears, and resources. The owners had high hopes that these projects would succeed.

We are talking about small, medium and large scale projects littered everywhere. These failed projects litter the world's landscape. They include partially completed or abandoned projects. Other failed projects include buildings, bridges, businesses, products, industries and many more. In most cases, colossal sums of money were spent to put them in place.

The owners would have avoided this mishap and failure had they sought the help and viewpoint of God before undertaking such projects. We believe they would have made it, had they spent adequate time to seek the Lord and find the will and heart of God about it. The Lord would have made known His will in the matter. Their story would have concluded favorably.

This helps us understand that it is always important to seek, do, and fulfill only those things that line up with the purpose of God for our lives. We have to come to the place where only the purpose of God for our lives consumes us.

Chapter 3

We Are Not Created To Be Ordinary

We (humans) are not ordinary beings. We are spirit beings created in the image of God. We are spirit beings before we are human beings. We have a soul and we live in a body. Our body can be likened to a container.

God created the first man Adam from the dust of the earth, and then breathed into him, so it is written; *"The first man Adam became a living being"* (1 Corinthians 15:45, Genesis 2:7). And Adam became a living being (Hebrew; *nephesh*), with a psyche; emotions, mind, and will, but yet subject to decay and corruption. The Lord Jesus is declared as the last Adam. Yet, Jesus Christ, the last Adam has become a life-giving Spirit, (Hebrew; *ruach*, Greek; *pneuma*) (vs 45). The Lord

God created us a living being with spirit, soul, and body. Our extraordinary identity is further elaborated;

> *The spiritual did not come first, but the natural, and after that the spiritual. The first man was of the dust of the earth; the second man is of heaven. As was the earthly man, so are those who are of the earth; and as is the heavenly Man, so also are those who are of heaven. And just as we have borne the image of the earthly man, so shall we bear the image of the heavenly man* (1 Corinthians 15:46-48).

The Holy Scriptures help us understand who we are and where we are heading. We are from God, created by Him. We have the soul and spirit He has given us. We will finally return to Him. Between, we have choices and options. We have to look up to his choices, options and purpose for us and diligently obey them. There are plenty of Scriptures that help us know and believe that we are not ordinary at all. Above all they urge us not to live an ordinary life, but as our Creator purposed us. In our identity;

- We are children of God the Most High, the Almighty, the King of Kings and Lord of Lords (John 1:12-13, Romans 8:15
- We have a future and a hope (Jeremiah 29:11)

- We are loved by God the Father (John 3:16, 1 John 3:1)
- We are created in the image of God (Genesis 1:27)
- We have the mind of God (1 Corinthians 2:16)
- We are seated with Christ in heavenly places (Ephesians 2:6)
- We are blessed with every spiritual blessings in Christ Jesus (Ephesians 1:3)
- We lack no good thing, we have everything we need for life godliness and devotion (2 Peter 1:3)
- We are God's handiwork, created in Christ Jesus to do good works, which God prepared in advance for us to do (Ephesians 2:10)
- We are partakers of (participants in) the divine nature of God (2 Peter 1:4).

We Are Supernatural Beings

Whereas we have a physical body, there is supernatural life inside of us. The life-giving spirit that we have in us (*ruach, nephesh, pneuma*), enables us understand that we are not ordinary. In the entire book of Acts, we see that after the apostles and disciples received the Holy Spirit, they began to perform extraordinary acts as the Lord Jesus had prophesied. This truth and others in His word make us realize that we are so precious and valuable to Father God.

The truths help us to live with courage and hope. We are not created to be ordinary. We realize that we are more precious than other creatures. We are further convinced that we are more precious than the various wonderful creations and inventions of mankind. There are many such examples. They include the wonderful high rise buildings, airplanes, cars, computers and many more. We possibly contributed to the fabrication of these marvelous works and inventions. We know that our brains function way better and faster than these inventions of man. Because our brains are better than the best of computers, we have confidence that with the help of God we can produce excellent results.

We ought to use these inventions to glorify God. We are an excellent piece of work of God. The apostle Paul tells us that, *"For we are God's handiwork, created in Christ Jesus to do good works, which God prepared in advance for us to do"* (Ephesians 2:10). The Lord who created us is interested in producing excellent results through us as we cooperate with him in the purpose He has for us. Not only do we have the Holy Spirit resident in us, but we are also the temple of God almighty. With the Spirit of God inside of us, we can achieve much. *"Do you not know that your bodies are temples of the Holy Spirit, who is in you, whom you have received from God? You are not your own; you were bought at a price"* (1 Corinthians 6:19-20). No other creature has this advantage.

We are seated with Christ in heavenly places. The apostle Paul in Ephesians 2: 6; tells us that; *"God raised us up with Christ and seated us with Him in the heavenly realms in Christ Jesus."* And we have all we need to live a godly life as clarified in Ephesians 1:3-4. While Peter the apostle teaches us that the divine power of God is available for us to lead a godly life. *"His divine power has given us everything we need for a godly life through our knowledge of him who called us by his own glory and goodness"* (2 Peter 1:3).

These facilities are not limited in scope but include what we need for life and godliness. They include spiritual, emotional, physical, financial and other requirements necessary for us to live a life of godliness and victory.

We Are Created To Do Great Exploits

With such encouragement, we come to know that we are shaped for victory when we carry out what God created us for (His purpose for our lives). This purpose, plans, and assignments are His. He does them through us. In reality, He accomplishes His plans through us, as His Holy Spirit inside of us directs us. Our main task is to cooperate, follow and obey the leading of His Holy

Spirit.

We are created to do great exploits (see Daniel 11:32), we can do all things through Christ who strengthens us (Philippians 4:13). We are so created that in the purpose, plan, and call of God for us, we have no chance of total failure. But when we are cut off from God we are in great trouble. *"I am the vine; you are the branches. If you remain in me and I in you, you will bear much fruit; apart from me, you can do nothing"* (John 15:5). This means that when we obey the purpose God created us for, we stand to produce good results. What we do blesses God and those He leads us to. In this way we contribute to the advancement of His kingdom and ultimately glorify Him. We play our part, and that is all we are required to do. How are we supernatural then?

As we use the gifts we received from God and the Holy Spirit, the splendor, greatness, and wonders of God are displayed. In the physical, we are able to see the manifestation of our supernatural nature as enabled by the Holy Spirit. Fortunately, some gifts of the Holy Spirit produce physical spectacular displays too. This helps produce faith in us and the non-believers too. However, we should not only be on the look-out for the spectacular displays. We ought to look for the evidence of the fruit of the Spirit as evidence of our changed lives and supernatural nature.

We Ought Not To Settle For Less

Something always tries to stop us from achieving our true potential. We tend to settle for less. So then we are not to settle for anything less, once we are aware of our significance in the design of Father God. We ought not to settle for a purpose or work that the Lord has not called us to do, a purpose that He did not create us for. Setbacks should not make us faint and give up.

We are encouraged by the tenacity of most athletes and other high achievers. These put in hours and train in exceptionally tough environments and terrain before they are crowned with medals. Even though they are engaged in worldly pursuits, we have a lot to learn from them.

The beauty is that it is the Lord's responsibility to support us to do His work. This helps us avoid the pride to believe falsely that we achieved the results in our strength. Instead we are enabled to keep on track knowing that He is with us to the very end of the age (Matthew 28:20). Our responsibility is to listen and obey. The Lord takes the responsibility to protect and provide for us as He promised in His word in Matthew 6:33. In this Scripture, the Lord promised that when we seek first His kingdom and His righteousness, all these things will be added unto us.

The things the Lord taught about included

material things that stress and grieve many daily. We believe they do include food, clothing, shelter, education, health (Medicare), money for bills, and many more. We stand secure because the Lord and His word cannot fail. The bible tells us in John 10:35 that scripture cannot be broken, and in the book of Psalms, that God has exalted above all things His word and His Name (Psalm 138:2). His word is eternal, it stands firm in the heavens. The Lord keeps His promises, and cannot bring His mighty Name into disrepute.

Pursue The Purpose Of God

We come from God and are going back to Him. In between our entry and departure, He has a beautiful purpose for us to fulfill. What makes us live a life of un-Christian strife often boils down to the fact that we have not found the purpose of God for our lives. Sometimes, this is not our wish, either. We find ourselves in this situation, due to lack of knowledge. No one showed us what to do. This is the prime reason. Scripture tells us that we are destroyed for lack of knowledge, yet this knowledge was available, but hidden from us (Hosea 4:6).

Had we known this truth that God has a specific purpose for us, we would have sought the Lord with all our hearts. We would then have found and carried out the purpose of God for us. Yet this does not mean that we may be involved in some evil or criminal undertaking and if so we ought to abandon such. In fact, we may be sincere and committed Christians. We may be involved in a very sane and legally profitable undertaking. Except that things do not seem to work for us, and we wonder why. We are most likely highly successful, by the measurement and ranking of the world. The world's perspective on things is not always necessarily the same as the Lord's perspective. We do not judge anybody, except pray that each person finds the purpose and call of God for their lives.

The flip side is that you may be someone who knows with certainty the purpose, mission, and call of God for your life. Except that you may be hesitant to do it. As long as you are alive you can repent and get right back on track, and the Lord will enable you to achieve results. The prophet Jonah, King David, the apostle Paul, Moses, and many others did the same. The last three were involved in murder of innocent people at some point or aided it. The scriptures tell us that Paul (Saul) approved of the murder of the early Christians. The Lord forgave them and restored them because of His unconditional love and mercy. They too repented on their part.

You probably know the purpose the Lord created you for, but due to fear or some other hindrances, you have not taken off. The other lamentable cases regard those that tried, but due to the cares of this world, the lures of wealth and other passions and desires, decided to quit. Such are encouraged to get right back where they started with God. We are consoled to find that the Lord is ready to take us back. We know with certainty that God is a gracious God of mercy and love. And as in the parable of the prodigal son, the Lord is gracious to receive us back in His fold.

Chapter 4

Take Steps To Find Your Purpose

We only live once on earth, and we want to ensure that we live fulfilled lives. We do not want to regret the race we ran, or what we achieved, spiritually, emotionally and materially. This is possible when we pursue and receive the wisdom and counsel of God to do this. We require not only the truth of God's word, but also, knowledge, wisdom, insight, and foresight to do this. We realize that we need power, and a sound mind to do this. We want to know and stay connected to this power source to help us do the purpose of God. When we discover this truth and take steps to obey and do the purpose of God for our lives, we are transformed. We receive energy, wisdom, courage, strength and faith to do it, and live our lives to the full.

The Lord Desires To Reveal His Purpose For Us

The Lord is more than interested to reveal to us His purpose for our lives, and He is ready to work with us to fulfill it. He patiently waits for us to receive it. Whereas we have a free will, He loves to partner with us and carry out His will instead. He will continue to remind us in some way about this important plan of his. This is foretold in the book of the prophet Jeremiah thus; *"For I know the plans I have for you, declares the Lord, plans to prosper you and not to harm you, plans to give you hope and a future. Then you will call on me and come and pray to me, and I will listen to you. You will seek me and find me when you seek me with all your heart"* (Jeremiah 29:11-13).

We have to cooperate with our loving Father in this important mission. Others may discourage us, but we know better. We have only one life and we do not want to reach the end of our lives with regret. This is something that should not happen to any sincere Christian whose desire is to please God and always live a life of victory. While on earth, our desire should be to run the proper race and win. We do this with the strength, wisdom, and grace of God.

We Have The Greatest Chance Of Victory

The purpose chosen by God for us is where

we have the greatest chance of victory. The Lord knows us too well, and purposed to only involve us in assignments we are able to do. He equips us and creates upfront the necessary conditions we need to succeed. So we do not have to be afraid.

When we cooperate with the Lord the entire heaven is on our side. In the story of the prophet Elisha in 2 Kings 6:8-23, we learn how the prophet had the help of hosts of angels supporting him in the work of God. The prophet Elisha received angelic and heavenly help all the time. Being a prophet this was not unusual to him. However, it seemed very unusual to his assistant, who had no idea that his master the prophet operated this way. In those days the King of Aram wanted to capture the prophet Elisha, and the king sent a strong force of horses and chariots. These surrounded the city and the prophet by night.

Early next morning this assistant of the prophet, upon waking up, saw and realized that enemy forces had surrounded them. Alarmed he reported this fact to his boss, the prophet. The prophet calmly told him, "Don't be afraid," And added, "Those who are with us are more than those who are with them." And Elisha prayed, "Open his eyes, Lord, so that he may see." Then the Lord opened the servant's eyes, and he immediately beheld an army of chariots and horses of fire from heaven to protect him and the prophet.

Elisha had more superior angelic and

heavenly help than the Arameans. His servant was amazed to see the heavenly army available to help him and the prophet Elisha. Moreover, the prophet already knew that in an amazing move, the Lord would enable him to daze the Arameans with partial blindness and trap them. It all worked out to the advantage of the prophet.

This constant angelic help was available to Elisha. Why? This is a man who was sold out in doing the purpose, call and will of God for his life, and the nation of Israel. Once, we are in the purpose and call of God we have the help of God and the angelic hosts of heaven to see us through. God's help is always available to us, even though we may not physically "see it".

Not All Are Called To The Ordained Purpose

We may seek clarification as to whether the purposes and calls of God are for laypersons too. Are not the purposes, plans, and calls intended for the apostles, prophets, evangelists, pastors, priests and teachers only? We may say; I am a layperson or a businessperson engaged somewhere else already. I am striving hard to make money and keep my kids and family alive, and I thought that calls and purposes are for specific people engaged in church work? Was I not just relegated to live the ordinary life and get by? The quick answer is that we are all created to fulfill some specific purpose of God.

You would not have been created if the Lord had no purpose for you to fulfill. You are possibly called to the non-ordained service to the people of God as the majority are. This is termed as the call to the marketplace. You may be involved in an assignment despised by people, and this can be a perfect work that glorifies God, for example, you may be involved in supporting orphans or street children.

Whatever the Lord has assigned us to do is equally important in advancing His kingdom. His vineyard is too vast (Luke 10:2) and requires numerous workers. *"For the eyes of the Lord run to and fro throughout the whole earth, to show Himself strong on behalf of those whose heart is loyal to Him"* (1 Chronicles 16:9).

The Lord continually searches for those willing to co-labor with Him. In the book of the prophet Isaiah, The Lord sought someone to co-labor with. He asked around, saying "Whom shall I send?" Isaiah accepted after some hesitation. The Lord cleansed him and equipped him to start work. *"See, this has touched your lips; your guilt is taken away and your sin atoned for." Then I heard the voice of the Lord saying, "Whom shall I send? And who will go for us?" And I said, "Here am I. Send me!"* (Isaiah 6:8).

Moses and Jeremiah hesitated too, with Jonah taking off in the opposite direction. Today we know and regard these prophets with esteem. The other elect of God; apostles, prophets, evangelists, pastors, priests, teachers are equally called. They too have their purpose and role to play. We may see them as more favored and prominent. Perhaps God sees them this way too, perhaps not. We love them and pray for them. They help and nurture us continually, we owe much to them. They have a special relationship and contact with the Lord, and it is all for our benefit.

We can lean on them. We ought to support them. We especially need to learn from their victory against severe odds. The Lord protects and keeps them safe and afloat. This is despite severe storms and circumstances that beset them all through the ages. Things seem to be working well for them. They rarely lack or fail which helps us to understand the significance of co-laboring with God in the purpose He created us for. They are a great example to learn from. God truly cares for them.

Similarly, we too should be wise to seek, find, accept and do the purpose of God for our lives. As an example, we do not want to be a successful engineer, carpenter or businessperson when we are created to be a nurse, social worker or gospel teacher. We would be a misfit and despite any success to our record, we would fail to find fulfillment and peace in our lives. We should not struggle to be an apostle, priest or prophet when we are called to serve as a social worker or nurse. We risk running into trouble since the graces required to triumph in such a purpose is not available or sufficient for us. Why strive to be a sheep when you are a goat?

It is possible to start at a humble step in the purpose and move up as the Lord pleases. Scripture records that the apostle Paul at one point was a teacher and prophet (Acts 13:1). We should not despise a lowly start. Possibly we will start from the bottom on a slow journey on the right path. God is not limited in his ways. Furthermore, do not be surprised that you are fulfilling more than one purpose at a go. It means that you have the grace and ability. This should be all right since you are created and equipped to succeed that way.

There Are Steps To Take

When we refuse to accept our call and purpose, the Lord looks for someone else to replace us. In the book of first Samuel after King Saul rebelled against God, he was eventually replaced by King David. Until the time of our death, this purpose of God for our lives will still hold. *"For God's gifts and his call are irrevocable"* (Romans 11:29).

When we accept and embrace the purpose and call of God for us, after this lapse, the Lord restores us. We are restored to achieve our purpose in a way and mode the Lord deems fit. Our purposes are supernatural and thus we may not find them by the use of the motivational coaching methods. We have to go to God or His servants to help us.

There are steps to take to realize this goal and we have to cooperate with God to see this come to pass. The Lord requires our agreement and obedience. Others may discourage us, but we know better. We do not want to reach the end of our life and discover rather late that we ran the wrong race. There is a specific race marked out for us as described in the book of Hebrews 12:1.

Also, we do not want to engage in works that burn up (has not much credit in the eyes of God). As described in the metaphor by Paul the apostle, they burn up due to our use of inappropriate methods and materials, being found to be of wood, hay or straw (see 1 Corinthians 3:15). We need not despair because the Lord who started this good work promised to bring it to completion.

The apostle Paul was convinced likewise, he said, *"I thank my God every time I remember you. In all my prayers for all of you, I always pray with joy because of your partnership in the gospel from the first day until now, being confident of this, that he who began a good work in you will carry it on to completion until the day of Christ Jesus"* (Philippians 1:6). This type of work does not burn up.

Chapter 5

Purpose Starts With Our Transformation

At times we come to a place where our personal dreams are shattered and nothing seems to work. We seem to have come to the end of the road. No door seems to be open. We ought to rejoice and see this as a great opportunity. It means that a new and open door is at hand. It is time for us to find and enter into new opportunities. The Lord is reinventing us. We are being shaped for a better place and assignment.

When we lose opportunities there has to be a better one. This is the time to persist and seek the right opportunity, and not go back to a futile purpose. It is an excellent time to seek the Lord to reveal to us what we can do that glorifies Him the most. This is a welcome situation to seek and enter the purpose and will of God for us.

We know that nothing happens on earth without the knowledge of the loving Father. God reigns and is concerned not only about us. He is in fact even concerned about birds of all types, and about all that He created. This scripture very well describes it, *"Are not two sparrows sold for a penny? Yet not one of them will fall to the ground outside your Father's care. And even the very hairs of your head are all numbered"* (Matthew 10:29-30).

The Lord cares about sparrows and all the other bird species and creatures. He is concerned when something happens to them, for example when any of them falls to the ground or dies. As one man once said, the Lord attends the funeral of sparrows. So what about us His children, created in His image? We can be certain that the Lord takes care of us too.

Any unfavorable circumstance should help us evaluate our relationship with God. Rather than mark them as odd, we should use these as opportunities to restore any broken relationship with Him. We have to listen to the voice of God during these times with greater humility, reverence, and sensitivity. And recognize and obey what the Lord is telling us. The Lord must have brought us to such a season to prepare us to cross into His purpose and plans for our lives. God speaks to us also through such moments and circumstances. The events in the life of the church in Philadelphia indicated an open door. In the book of Revelation 3:8; the angel to that church announced that a door had opened for them. The angel told them, *"see I have opened before you a door that no one can close"* (Revelation 3:8).

When we come to a place where doors close and others open we have to be grateful to the Lord. We have to prayerfully seek God for His direction. Other circumstances require us to wait. This prepares us for the oncoming opportunity. We are not to stay stagnant, even at this waiting stage-but put our hands to something. The Lord wants us to grow during this time. The challenges and circumstances strengthen our perseverance and character. A failure in one field is not the end. It signals the start of a new phase.

Our Transformation Is Being Worked Out

As we reflect and seek God, He guides us. These shape us for subsequent assignments. The reflection helps us understand the perspective of God. The Holy Spirit enables us to see things with spiritual eyes, the eyes of faith. We are able to see His perspective in it and the Lord working everything for our good. What was dim becomes clearer.

We learn from the example of the apostles and disciples, who initially had a hazy view of the mission of Christ. The passion, crucifixion, and death of our Lord Jesus Christ seemed awful. To the disciples, it seemed to be a total irredeemable loss. They scattered in many geographical areas. They imagined a Christ who should have restored Israel from the political domination of Rome. They asked Him directly if he was at that time going to restore the kingdom to Israel (Act 1:6-8). His answer was yes, but not in the way they imagined. He said to them: *"It is not for you to know the times or dates the Father has set by his own authority. But you will receive power when the Holy Spirit comes on you; and you will be my witnesses in Jerusalem, and in all Judea and Samaria, and to the ends of the earth."*

The Holy Spirit was to enable them to witness and create a new Kingdom in the entire world. They would capture greater territory than they imagined. The point here is that there is the perspective of God in all things that we often cannot grasp easily. Yet when all seemed to have failed according to the disciples, a new dawn and everlasting empire that would save entire humanity emerged.

The Lord's passion, crucifixion, death, and resurrection glorified God and brought salvation to all mankind. When they received the Holy Spirit their eyes were opened and they received power, boldness, strength, courage, and wisdom to fulfill the mission Jesus assigned them. Our painful loss and suffering is an important stage to move into the purpose of God.

We Have Not Lost Everything

We at times think that we have lost all. When we lose everything we still have the Lord Jesus by our side. We gain everything since we do not have anything more to lose. We gain our Lord and Savior Jesus. We can start afresh with the Lord. The apostle Paul had the same experience. He said *"But whatever were gains to me I now consider loss for the sake of Christ. What is more, I consider everything a loss because of the surpassing worth of knowing Christ Jesus my Lord, for whose sake I have lost all things"* (Philippians 3:7-8).

There will be downturns in many facets of life. There are economic downturns, depressions and such. Personal misfortunes and downturns often occur. These losses provide an opportunity to reach out to our God who is bigger than all the troubles around.

There is no such thing as failure in God's kingdom. Father God has decided to use hopeless situations to bring good. He uses the weak, the undesirable, the rejects, the foolish, the disqualified in the eyes of the world to accomplish His purpose (1 Corinthians 1:26-30). And whoever comes to Jesus, He never drives away (John 6:37). The loss of a job or failure of your business is an example of only one door closing. As one door closes others open for you to move to the next level for the greater glory of God. We should receive both with gratitude. The apostle Paul tells us in 1 Thessalonians 5:18, to give thanks in all circumstances, saying that giving thanks is the will of God in Christ Jesus. The closed-door "opens us up" and frees us to the infinite possibilities in God's vineyard.

Father God has opened up his vast vineyard to "whosoever" will come and co-labor with Him. Closed doors are an opportunity to enter and serve in the vast vineyard of the Lord. *"He told them, "The harvest is plentiful, but the workers are few. Ask the Lord of the harvest, therefore, to send out workers into his harvest field"* (Luke 10:2).

There Is No Unemployment In God's Kingdom

This helps us understand that there exists infinite opportunities in the vineyard of the Lord. God has much work lying undone, and He is searching for workers. When we seek and find our place in this grand scheme of God, we contribute to the advancement of His kingdom.

In other cases, we are called to step in and do the work that someone else declined to do or mishandled. This happened to King David. The prophet Samuel anointed him to do what King

Saul failed to do. As a result of disobedience, the Lord rejected King Saul. Judas Iscariot was replaced by Mathias. And Peter, the apostle realized to his amazement, that Father God is no respecter of persons. He uses and works with anyone from any nation who fears and obeys Him. Even the pagans or gentiles are called to work in the vineyard of the Lord. In Acts 10:34-35, Peter began to speak, and said; *"I now realize how true it is that God does not show favoritism, but accepts from every nation the one who fears him and does what is right."*

Peter found out in the most unusual way, that the disqualified and the downtrodden are now chosen. His experience at Cornelius house set the stage for the conversion of the gentiles. The disqualified and downtrodden persons have a chance to rise to great levels of victory and achievement when they cooperate and obey God. All they need to do is to seek, know, obey and walk in the purpose of God for their lives. The poverty-stricken persons, tribes, and clans need not lose hope. They too need to seek and find the purpose of God for their lives and walk in obedience to fulfill it. And as they walk in the purpose of God and divine wisdom, the poverty spirit over them will be broken.

Much of the poverty in the world has its roots in broken fellowship with God. Poverty is first spiritual and its roots can be traced to a broken fellowship with God. And that is part of the reason why it has persisted for a long time. Secular authorities find it difficult to define or understand it. Secular books find no clear definition for it, neither do they propose a definitive way to stamp it out forever. They often describe it as "a complex concept, complex phenomena". When in reality, it is a spiritual state of brokenness. It manifests in the natural as persistent lack, a broken physical and material condition.

This broken relationship leads most people to live outside the planned purpose of God for their lives. This comes with the loss of grace to overcome the challenges that are common to all. To address it at its root, one has to look to God for the solution. One has to seek God earnestly, discern the cause and the source, break its roots and find and carry out the purpose and plan of God for their lives.

Temporary lack, hunger, or fasting, is certainly beneficial, and teaches us a lot. However, persistent and dire poverty, hunger, famine, deprivation is not the will of God for any of His children. We overcome such when we cooperate with God and receive His wisdom, and grace to overcome them. We have to believe and obey God, grow in faith and follow up with practical action. This has to be in line with an idea, vision, creativity or concept that the Lord shows us. This idea, concept or creativity has to come from Him.

We have to seek it from Him. The place to receive such is when we carry out the purpose of God for our lives.

Sanctification Is Part Of Our Call

Our sanctification is part of our call. It is one of the major stages in the purpose and call of God for our lives. The purpose of God requires us to pursue holiness. This is the answer to the meaning of life. This is not to say that we would have achieved perfection in holiness. What this means is that we reach a point where the Lord can trust us with His purpose. This is the point where our hearts desire what God desires. We are more interested to obey and follow what the Lord tells us more than ever before. The opinions and counsels of others are only received in so far as they line up with that of God. We are ready to co-operate with God in His purpose for us.

Dot By Dot

When the Lord is pleased with our obedience he will reveal His purpose for our lives. The Lord then gives us plans and instructions in bits that make practical sense, and which we can handle at a time. Our progress will be as the prophet Isaiah described *"For it is: Do this, do that, a rule for this, a rule for that, a little here, a little there"*

(Isaiah 28:10). Some people, however, will receive a much bigger chunk at a time. This happens to those with whom the Lord is greatly pleased with their past level of obedience. This happens to the people the Lord trusts greatly. For example Moses, Joshua and David were by and large faithful to the plans of God.

As we obey the Lord, He reveals to us subsequent portions of His purpose for us. The Lord gives us enough light for the moment to help us move ahead in the path for us. This is captured in Psalm 119:105, where the Psalmist tells us *"your word is a lamp for my feet, a light on my path"*. We will most times only have enough light to see us through. The Israelites in the desert were led by the hand of the Lord on all matters. *"By day the Lord went ahead of them in a pillar of cloud to guide them on their way and by night in a pillar of fire to give them light, so that they could travel by day or night. Neither the pillar of cloud by day nor the pillar of fire by night left its place in front of the people"* (Exodus 13: 21-22).

When we follow the leading of the Lord we will not fail to do the purpose the Lord has assigned for us. And even when we falter, while engaged in doing His mission, He restores us. He gets us back on track when we obey His word and cooperate with Him. What is important is that we should be somewhere along the path. Within our path (purpose), there is room for mistakes, although we should not commit them knowingly. The patriarchs Abraham, Moses, David, Elijah, Paul, and Peter made mistakes while within the purpose of God. They were all restored.

Only A Little Light On Our Path

We often wonder why the Lord reveals only a limited portion of our assignment at a time. We have to work with at most times scanty future details. This is because, if the entire plan is unveiled to us at once, it would scare and overwhelm us. Some would become paralyzed through fear, and freeze or freak out. We would have little room for creativity too. We would have to abide by stricter constraints if the Lord made the plans detailed.

That is what happened on Mount Sinai where the Lord spoke and gave the commands. It was spoken so clearly and with great miraculous signs and wonders. The result is that no one can go against those commands and not stray. Besides, wc could achieve a lot in a shorter timeframe, and become proud and take the glory for ourselves. We have to know that the purpose of the Lord for our lives has to do with advancing His kingdom. We may outrun others whose plans and assignments are tied to ours.

The Lord makes His plans flexible to take care of all these eternal setups, occasioned by our failures. We have to work with whatever the Lord has revealed or made known. More is revealed as and when we accomplish previous plans shown to us. We have just enough light for our feet and some light along the path.

Chapter 6

Be Conformed To The Likeness Of Christ

We have to be set apart as Holy to the purpose of God. We must join our lives to that of Christ to achieve this. Paul the apostle reminds us in his letter to the Corinthians to sanctify ourselves; *"dear friends, let us purify ourselves from everything that contaminates body and spirit, perfecting holiness out of reverence for God"* (2 Corinthians 7:1). To sanctify means to "set apart, or declare holy, purify, free from sin, cleanse". Whatever, is set apart is purified to be used for its intended purpose. We should continually commit and aim to live a holy life, and this is not a very easy thing.

Sanctification comes by abiding in Christ, which comes by obedience to Christ, and the leadership of the Holy Spirit. John the apostle emphasized that this is possible when we obey the commandments of God and thus remain in the love of God. John the apostle explained how this is possible;

> *Remain in me, as I also remain in you. No branch can bear fruit by itself; it must remain in the vine. Neither can you bear fruit unless you remain in me. "I am the vine; you are the branches. If you remain in me and I in you, you will bear much fruit; apart from me you can do nothing. If you do not remain in me, you are like a branch that is thrown away and withers; such branches are picked up, thrown into the fire and burned. If you remain in me and my words remain in you, ask whatever you wish, and it will be done for you. This is to my Father's glory, that you bear much fruit, showing yourselves to be my disciples. "As the Father has loved me, so have I loved you. Now remain in my love. If you keep my commands, you will remain in my love, just as I have kept my Father's commands and remain in his love* (John 15:4-11).

The bottom line is to remain in Christ and be led by the Holy Spirit. How do we remain in Christ? We do this by joining our life with His, by committing from deep within our heart to obey and follow Him in spite of our weaknesses. The starting point is our heart and its posture. If they could cut out your heart and read aloud what is in your heart, what would the script read like? God knows what is in our hearts (1 Samuel 16:7; 1 Chronicles 28:9).

Thereafter, our physical actions, our deeds ought to be in that direction. The Holy Spirit helps us in our daily efforts and enables us to hear what God is speaking, what God wants us to do. When we remain in obedience we are transformed from inside out. The spontaneous work of the Holy Spirit in us then produces in us visible character traits and attributes that are found in the nature of Christ. These are referred to as the fruit of the Holy Spirit. We must join our lives to that of Christ to achieve this.

Overcoming Hindrances To The Purpose Of God

There are several hindrances to following Christ and to our sanctification. We can overcome these by the power of Christ. We have the power and authority to overcome these hindrances in Christ; *"I have given you authority to trample on snakes and scorpions and to overcome all the power of the enemy; nothing will harm you"* (Luke 10:19).

These snakes and scorpions come in all forms. They only thrive and harm us when we give them ground, when we allow and consent to them knowingly or unknowingly. They are spiritual attacks of the enemy that eventually manifest in the natural when not resisted. James in his epistle helps us know how to deal with these hindrances, *"Submit yourselves, then, to God. Resist the devil, and he will flee from you. Come near to God and he will come near to you"* (James 4:7-8).

We have to develop a close relationship with God and do our part to resist the devil and the Lord will support us in our battles with the enemy. King David overcame Goliath the Philistine champion by coming against him in the name of the Lord. King David told Goliath, *"You come against me with sword and spear and javelin, but I come against you in the name of the Lord Almighty, the God of the armies of Israel, whom you have defied"* (1 Samuel 17: 45).

We ought to determine to follow the Lord with all our hearts and grow in faith, hope and love and the fruit of the Holy Spirit. These fruit (read as fruits) are often listed as nine but in reality, are various. They correspond to the level of transformation taking place in us. They help us know that the Holy Spirit is working internally, as we cooperate to produce tangible fruits aligned with the nature of God.

The lack of such fruit, help us know that we need to yield specific areas of our lives to God to conform to the image of Christ. Ephesians 2 and Galatians 3 encourages us to live in the righteousness that comes by grace and faith. Thus, if we are offended by anyone we ought not to seek recourse to the law or revenge. It is best for us to find a Christian way of love and forgiveness to solve the problem. We ought not stop at the law, but go beyond it. The law should point us to Christ, and grace requires us to live as a better and higher Christian witness compared to one living under the law. Through such severe tests, we develop the fruit of the Spirit.

Growth In The Fruit Of The Holy Spirit

The fruit of the Holy Spirit, (see Galatians 5:22) or the lack of it, is a good starting point to help us gauge our level of growth in our love and fellowship with God. The fruit of the Spirit are the attributes received from the Holy Spirit as a result of abiding in Christ. We start with love (Greek; agape). This love is a gift and nature of God. God is love and we too are commanded to live in love. Love is a gift, fruit, and the greatest commandment.

Paul the apostle teaches us that "agape" love is patient, kind. It does not envy, it does not boast, it is not proud. It does not dishonor others, it is not self-seeking, it is not easily angered, it keeps no record of wrongs. This kind of love does not delight in evil but rejoices with the truth. It always protects, always trusts, always hope and always perseveres. This love never fails.

The other fruits of the Spirit are Joy (Greek; *Chara*). Joy enables us to live in durable inner gladness and thanksgiving to God. And peace (Greek; *eirene*); is the internal peace that surpasses understanding. This peace is evident in us when we no longer live a life dominated and ruled by fear, worry, stress, and anxiety.

The others are patience, forbearance (Greek; *makrothumia* and Greek; *hupomone*), is explained as the courage and patience in adverse sufferings, patient endurance, long-suffering, forbearance and non recourse to revenge. While kindness (Greek; *Chrestotes*), is when we develop a sweetness of disposition to others. Further, we are friendly to others, gentle in dealing with others, generous, and considerate and affable.

More fruit includes; goodness (Greek; *agathosune*), as in uprightness of heart, kindness and doing good things. Faithfulness (Greek; *pistis*) involves trustfulness and dependability in matters and reliability. Also, in this case, we trust and believe in God and His promises. Gentleness (Greek; *prautes*), includes meekness, control of temper and passions, and mildness of disposition. And self-control (Greek; *egkrateia*) considers control of one's thoughts and actions, including control of sexual appetites, mental and physical chastity, and moderation in eating and drinking.

The Lord Jesus completed our redemption and waits for us to take daily steps to grow in Him, *"All those the Father gives me will come to me, and whoever comes to me I will never drive away "* (John 6:37), and *"If you remain in me and my words remain in you, ask whatever you wish, and it will be done for you. This is to my Father's glory, that you bear much fruit, showing yourselves to be my disciples"* (John 15:7-8).

When we come to Christ we become new creatures (see 2 Corinthians 5:17) and partakers of divine nature (2 Peter 1:4). Paul the apostle explains that we start our long journey of sanctification when we receive Christ and abide in Him.

The Lord Jesus became the sacrificial lamb, and overcome all the limitations and hindrances to our friendship with God. Paul helps us understand the finished work of the Lord Jesus that is freely available to us. Ephesians 1:7; *"In him, we have redemption through his blood, the forgiveness of sins, in accordance with the riches of God's grace that he lavished on us. With all wisdom and understanding, he made known to us the mystery of his will according to his good pleasure, which he purposed in Christ, to be put into effect when the times reach their fulfillment— to bring unity to all things in heaven and on earth under Christ".*

Overcoming Our Sins And Those Of Our Ancestors

We live in a time of immense grace, and love and mercy of God. This helps us understand that the requirements are higher than that of the law. We have a better covenant with better promises to take advantage of. The Lord Jesus overcame sin, death, poverty, sickness and disease on our behalf.

Sin and other hindrances had been major obstacles until the Lord won the victory on our behalf, and saved us from them. Sin, rebellion, iniquity, and disobedience separate us from the love of God, and hinder our sanctification. We need to confess, repent, renounce, take responsibility and accept forgiveness for our sins, rebellions, iniquities and disobedience (and for those of our parents and ancestors). This restores the broken relationship with God.

And we are required to forgive and make amends with those we have wronged, and, those that have wronged us. This enables us to restore the broken relationship with them and God. We do not have time or space to hate anyone or hold bitterness against anyone. Whereas the Lord still loves us even when we fall, He waits for us to make the move to return to Him.

Sin (noun) is described as *"an immoral act considered a transgression against divine law."*

The main reason the Lord Jesus came down to earth was to save us from sins. He came to offer himself up as an eternal sacrifice to do away with sins. Hebrew 10: 12-14 teaches us that the Lord Jesus has redeemed us from our sins. *"But when this priest had offered for all time one sacrifice for sins, he sat down at the right hand of God, and since that time he waits for his enemies to be made his footstool". For by one sacrifice he has made perfect forever those who are being made holy".*

We have to confess and repent of all sins and we are restored to God, and move on. The other sins that require rigorous similar treatment are those of our parents and ancestors. We similarly need to confess, repent, renounce, take responsibility, seek and accept forgiveness for the sins of our fathers and ancestors. This is irrespective of whether they are alive or dead. The book of Lamentations helps us know that we bear the punishment for the sins, iniquities and rebellions of our ancestors. In the book of Lamentations, 5:7, we learn that *"Our ancestors sinned and are no more, and we bear their punishment".*

The effects of any generational sins and unhealed foundations need to be dealt with by us to enable grace to flow in that area. The Pharisees and the disciples of Jesus understood this principle quite well. They knew about generational sins; *"As he went along, he saw a man blind from birth. His disciples asked him, "Rabbi, who sinned, this man or his parents, that he was born blind?" "Neither this man nor his parents sinned," said Jesus, "but this happened so that the works of God might be displayed in him"* (John 9:1-3).

The remedy for all sins whether our own or that of our ancestors is to confess, renounce and repent of them. *"But if they will confess their sins and the sins of their ancestors—their unfaithfulness and their hostility toward me, which made me hostile toward them so that I sent them into the land of their enemies—then when their uncircumcised hearts are humbled and they pay for their sin, I will remember my covenant with Jacob and my covenant with Isaac and my covenant with Abraham, and I will remember the land"* (Leviticus 26:40-43).

The Lord God appeared to King Solomon twice during his lifetime. God discussed with King Solomon what He requires should be done if and when sin hampers their nation. The temple, though complex, had at its center the Holy of Holies, that contained the Ark of the Covenant. The Ark of the Covenant contained the Ten Commandments. On top of the Ark of the Covenant was the mercy seat, where Moses spoke directly with God, between the wings of the Cherubim. At the heart of the temple of God in Jerusalem, was God, the merciful God, who meets us at the mercy seat, and offers us mercy.

God counseled Solomon that four things would be required for the land and people to be healed, when they sinned. *"If my people, who are called by my name, will humble themselves and pray and seek my face and turn from their wicked ways, then I will hear from heaven, and I will forgive their sin and will heal their land"* (2 Chronicles 7:14). We are not held accountable for the sins of our ancestors. Neither should we judge our ancestors. However, the effect and consequences of their sins, iniquities and rebellion are experienced to this day. And the effects are seen in almost everyone, to varying degrees.

These patterns persist if not brought to Christ and dealt with. These continue to afflict suffering and pain to the present and subsequent generations. Galatians 3:13-14, teaches us that *"Christ redeemed us from the curse of the law by becoming a curse for us, for it is written: "Cursed is everyone who is hung on a pole". He redeemed us in order that the blessing given to Abraham might come to the Gentiles through Christ Jesus so that by faith we might receive the promise of the Spirit".*

We have to be alert to those areas in our lives that frequently and persistently show a negative pattern. Some sins never seem to go away from us. Some of the sins we struggle so hard to overcome are carried over from the heinous deeds of our parents and forefathers. And once repented of are completely overcome.

Other negative patterns due to the iniquities of our forefathers often manifest as; incurable diseases, sinfulness, failures, persistent poverty, barrenness, inability to marry, divorce, history of suicides, financial and business failures, lack of fruit-fullness, proneness to accidents, premature deaths, suicides, mental illness, and many others. These areas consistently post negative fruit of the Spirit. When we meet the conditions and appropriate what Christ has already done, we receive healing. We require the help of Christ to overcome them, and need to believe, pray, fast and repent. However, the starting point is faith. We have to grow in faith and believe that the Lord Jesus Christ has already fought and won the battle on our behalf.

Additional Areas For Healing

There are other areas to bring to the attention of the Lord Jesus for healing. We have to yield or surrender them for healing. These other areas often include trauma of all kinds. We have to forgive those that caused them (if any as some traumas do not dawn on us due to the direct fault of others) and ask the Lord Himself to heal the trauma and replace the bad, negative pictures, with those that heal us.

The others are, inner-vows (the remedy; repent and renounce them), ungodly or evil soul ties, (the remedy; we repent and break the ungodly soul ties in Jesus' Name), unbelief and ungodly belief (the remedy; repent and replace with godly truth, belief, and confessions), word curses, (the remedy; renounce, confess repent of the curse, forgive those that caused it, and break the curse in Jesus Name).

While there are some more as below; These include bitterness and un-forgiveness (the remedy; forgive all involved, forgive yourself, and forgive God to repair your image of God). Unresolved anger requires repentance, and some anger has the spirit of murder at its roots. Thus, repent of murder. Further, we need to repent and get delivered from worry, fear, stress, anxiety.

There are other areas (often deep and hidden from us) that are often ignored such as wrong thinking, deception, rejection that requires similar treatment. These too need to be healed by Jesus. Thus, sanctification requires the help of the Lord Jesus and the Holy Spirit. It is a life-long process and requires our daily cooperation.

Chapter 7

Pointers To The Purpose Of God

Sometimes the purpose the Lord created us for is momentarily shown to us, but we simply cannot recognize it. We fail to keep it in remembrance or focus. Other times, we are aware of it, but we cannot make any sense of it. The apostle Paul found it difficult to understand why anyone could refuse to serve a loving, caring and merciful God. And instead, opt to serve someone else or at least place their loyalty somewhere else.

It was revealed to him that this happens as a result of a veil that the enemy places over our faces. This veil then covers our faces. This enemy is the adversary, Satan, the god of this age. The veil stops us from entering into the fullness of God as described by the apostle Paul in his letter to the Corinthians (2 Corinthians 3:14-15; 4:3-4). When this veil is removed we are then able to see the perspective of God for our lives.

Fortunately, this veil does not permanently cover the purpose of God for us. There are momentary glimpses and circumstances when it lifts off and those surrounding us can see through and figure out our gifts, purpose, and call. This is because the gifts and call of God are irrevocable (Romans 11:29). We are born with these gifts, and they stay with us, whether we put them to use or not.

We Need Determination And Courage

To find and recognize the purpose of God requires us to seek God for it with all our hearts. We need determination and courage. To seek in this sense means to use all godly means at our disposal to enable us to receive the answer. Such include recourse to prayer, reading, and the meditation on the word, of the bible and other holy books. We have to attend where possible seminars, and seek the godly counsel of people around us. And make use of other godly ways. As we press on through such means, the Lord eventually reveals His purpose to us.

God is more than willing to reveal His purpose to us. After all, that is why he created us. It is his greatest joy to see us live a fulfilled life. What he requires from us is a heart that is ready to receive. We must be ready before he reveals it. We need such determination and courage as Joshua had, to receive and know this important purpose of His (see Joshua 1: 6; 7; 9). The Lord and Moses encouraged Joshua.

Satan often convinces us that we are on the right track when we are not. Satan himself most times masquerades as an angel of light (2 Corinthians 11:14). In this case, light (and darkness) are metaphors and represent good and evil. However, there are often plain outward indicators and signs in a person's life that point towards the purpose of God for such a person. One such sign are our gifts. Take the example of a little kid of less than ten years (pre-teenager). Often a little kid of such a tender age is already an acclaimed pianist or organist, while a fully grown up person is figuring out what to do with their lives.

Words People Speak About Us

Those we meet often tell us "we have this or that quality or talents". As for any other prophecy, we have to crosscheck this and ask God to confirm it. Often such people only wish to flatter us, while others are insincere. The example of the child Jesus illustrates this point. Many people spoke amazing things about the child Jesus. The Scriptures tell us that Mary the mother of Jesus kept pondering the words people spoke about the child Jesus. She constantly wondered what kind of person the child Jesus would grow up to be. This is because most people kept saying amazing things about Jesus in her hearing. Thus we should not dismiss the words being spoken about us but rather ponder them. They may point out or directly show us the Lord's purpose for our lives. It is important to ponder them as Mary the mother of the Lord Jesus did.

The Circumstance Of Our Birth

We ought to inquire from our elders and parents about our birth. As happened to the Lord Jesus and John the Baptist some of the signs of our purpose were revealed at the time of our birth and childhood. We need to piece them together to discover what the Lord has already made known to our parents and those present. There are several people whose birth and early life story sound like a fairy tale or movie. This makes many to conclude that such persons are poised to do great things for God. Anyone in this category need not look back except to seek the Lord in earnest to find the purpose of God for their lives.

The circumstance of our birth and childhood is a unique pointer to the purpose and call of God for us. It is often said that everything happens for a purpose. Before the birth of John the Baptist, an angel of the Lord appeared to his father Zachariah. And before the birth of Jesus, the angel Gabriel was sent to the Virgin Mary in the town of Nazareth. Most of us have never seen an angel. The appearance and sighting of an angel at any point in our lives is a very significant event. When the Lord Jesus was born an angelic host of heaven spoke to the shepherds tending their sheep nearby, informing them about His birth.

These shepherds reported what the angels had told them to Mary and Joseph *"but Mary treasured up all these things and pondered them in her heart"* (Luke 2:19). Such distinct babies have distinct purposes. These have a degree of urgency and a somewhat short time frame.

Given this unique birth circumstance, John the Baptist did not have to figure out whether he would be a carpenter or a fisherman. We have to be on the outlook for unusual occurrences. Angels are pure spirits that carry messages of God. In our time, this may not necessarily be the visit of an angel or angels, but of people who speak unusual things about us, and predict our future. Often times the Lord gives words of wisdom to them, that they speak over us spontaneously and unexpectedly. These then are able to forctell our future and God's plans for us. They speak to us things that point us towards God, service to God and our influence.

Those Orphaned At Birth

Some people are orphaned at birth and live to see another day. There must be a divine reason for this. Growing motherless or parent-less is not pleasant. Others are born in poverty and struggle through life. Sometimes, those born in poverty promise or vow to succeed financially at all costs. Serving God may seem a hindrance to achieving this success. Growing parent-less or in poverty is a direct indication of the call of God as described in Matthew 5 in the beatitudes the Lord Jesus gave.

The absence of the god of mammon makes it easier to access the kingdom. However, those that vowed to come out of poverty, by all means, using their own devices, may have made an inner vow. Internally, they mean to access wealth even without the help of God. They need to renounce this inner vow and cooperate with God in His purpose for them. Wealth should not be their priority. The purpose of God should be. And in this way, the spiritual cause and source of this curse would be permanently broken by the Lord God.

In the sermon on the mountain recorded in the gospel of Matthew 5:3, the Lord Jesus invited the poor to enter the Kingdom. The beatitudes teach us that poverty is both a material and spiritual incapacitation. This helps us understand that when we come to the Kingdom, we receive graces and blessings to overcome both the spiritual and material poverty.

We may accumulate a fair amount of money and material possessions and yet remain spiritually poor. Who else can rescue us from such a situation? And what better way except to cooperate in the purpose of God for us. The materially poor and the materially wealthy ought to seek, find and do the purpose God created them for. When they do and follow the purpose of God for their lives the Lord will set them free from both spiritual and material poverty. The Lord has promised to free all from Satan's domination, and that includes spiritual and material poverty.

The invitation of Jesus is not limited to the poor, but to all others. They include those in dire circumstances like those handicapped, landless, classless, exiled, and refugee. While more cases relate to those who struggle and are unable to complete their education. Others struggle hard to achieve a limited level of education. These need not despair but should be encouraged to know that the Lord Jesus did not discriminate based on the level of education. He equally used the less educated apostles and disciples to do his work.

We applaud the support given to help those less fortunate than us. The Lord Jesus has decided to include even those born in less than ideal circumstances to take part in the work of his kingdom. In the kingdom of God, these have the favor of God to serve His high purpose and call. They need not look further. The Lord Jesus targeted all the unfortunate people in the world. His mission was to save and bring all into the Kingdom of God.

Those Who Survived Death

Anyone who survived death ought to thank God continually. There are many people out there who survived death at some point in their lives. This could have been occasioned through some freak accident, war, sickness, disease or infirmity, and other causes. And there are several others who survived death at birth or infancy. Their survival perplexed the best medical brains and surgeons who were present. "She/he has the least chance of making it", the medical officials concluded resignedly at that time.

There are a few others who died and came back to life. Some of these wonder as to what they should do next. These need to show gratitude to God and move on boldly and with joy to serve God in the purpose He has laid out for them. The Lord will show them what to do that fits their exceptional circumstances.

There are other circumstances that speak for themselves, and help us perceive that God is calling us to His purpose. They give us a glimpse into what the Lord desires us to pursue or do. These circumstances can be faint at the start and intensify till we act. As we seek the Lord about these, they become clearer. We do not have to dismiss them as of no consequence. We have to pray into them to see if they become stronger or diminish. The ones that evaporate may possibly not be what the Lord intended for us.

Chapter 8

How To Know The Purpose And Call Of God

The Holy Spirit reveals to us the purpose of God for our lives in several ways. The presence of peace is one of the evidence of the revelation of the purpose of God for our lives. When the purpose of God for our lives is revealed we will be filled with peace. This type of peace is difficult to explain, but we will know that we have it. This peace is the ruler, umpire, governor, safety, and guard of our heart.

The presence of this genuine peace is an indicator to us that we are in good standing with God. God speaks to us through the avenue of peace. The extreme lack of this peace is equally worth paying attention to. The lack of peace should help us know that there is something amiss. Paul tells us that; *"Let the peace of Christ rule in your hearts, since as members of one body you were called to peace, and be thankful"* (Colossians 3:15).

This peace (*eirene, pacis*) of God is received when we set our eyes on the things above where Christ is seated. It is a fruit of the Holy Spirit. The context of the third chapter of Colossians is to live and seek the will and higher things of God. We are promised this peace when we seek and find the purpose and call of God for us. When we do not find peace in our current engagements it is time to seek the Lord about it.

Our discomfort and desire for change help us seek God for the solution. The apostle Paul described peace as an empire, ruler, and governor. The peace is compared to the compass and navigational instrument the Holy Spirit has placed inside of us. This peace or lack of it helps us know whether we are on the right track or not. When we feel persistent disquiet in our spirit we ought to seek and ascertain the cause and find a way out. It is not a bad thing.

We should be grateful to God for the disquiet in our spirit. It is a positive indicator that our conscience is alive about this particular case. This disquiet disappears as soon as we find the purpose and assignment of the Lord for our lives.

Purpose Revealed By The Laying On Of Hands

The laying on of hands is an effective way by which the Holy Spirit reveals to us our gifts, plans, and purposes. When done by the right people it is very effective. Thus we have to ensure that we only submit to the rightful ceremonies. There are many cases in Scripture where those the Lord called were commissioned by the laying on of hands.

This happened in the Old Testament and the New Testament. For example, during the commissioning of Joshua, the Lord said to Moses; *"Take Joshua son of Nun, a man in whom is the spirit of leadership and lay your hand on him"* (Numbers 27:18). This happened after Moses had asked God to reveal who would succeed him. Paul the apostle said this to Timothy, *"For this reason, I remind you to fan into flame the gift of God, which is in you through the laying on of my hands"* (2 Timothy 1:6).

Timothy received this gift through a prophetic message when the body of elders laid their hands on him (1 Timothy 4:14). The laying on of hands commissions us to serve God. This gives us boldness to use the gifts we received from the Holy Spirit. And we learn in this case how Timothy was commissioned and began to function in his gift to the benefit of the believers around him. As a result of the laying on of hands upon him, he had the confidence and boldness to operate in the gifts he received.

We ought to look back and bring to remembrance when the right authorities laid hands on us. What was it for? What was that occasion meant to achieve? We may discover that the Lord commissioned us that day to start fulfilling His purpose for our lives. Yet unfortunately, we downplayed it and to this very day, we have not started. Those that laid hands on us are equally perplexed as to why up to now we have not started. At times we might have been afraid to start, or overwhelmed or skipped the preparatory stage. Other times we possibly had the knowledge and vision but did not pray through the vision we received.

Purpose Revealed In Phases

The apostle Paul started work as a teacher and ended up as an apostle (Acts 13:1). This helps us understand that in some instances there is a step by step gradation of the purpose and call of God. We may start at one level and end up at another level. There are often calls within a call.

Paul, the apostle was a prophet as we realize in this verse. Yet, we know him more for his work as an apostle, with miracles, signs, and wonders following him wherever he went. However, we see Paul involved in several other assignments. He was a teacher, preacher, and author. We learn here that Paul was blessed by God with various gifts, calls, skills, and offices. He was also a businessman. He often made tents (as did Priscilla and Aquila) for sale to customers.

This example of Paul encourages us to seek God to show us creative ideas and concepts we can use to earn income. This can be a business, or an undertaking, as long as it is godly and shown to us by Him. The progression, takes time, as we grow in faithfulness, obedience, and maturity. We do not have to limit God, even if, we may not function in several gifts.

Purpose Revealed By Seeking God

We have to seek the Lord earnestly through prayer, meditation, and any other holy avenue for Him to reveal to us what He created us for. Ask, seek and knock (Matthew 7:7). This is not going to take anyone a day or two or some few days, as initially all that the Lord does is to transform us. For the majority this remains the only way to find the purpose of God for their lives.

The revelation of the purpose of God for our lives starts with our transformation. To receive the purpose of God for our lives we have to set our hearts firmly on the things of God, to pursue God as our priority. It is the call to sanctification, holiness and right standing with God.

It is the call for everyone. The call to holiness is not only a call but also the will of God in Christ Jesus, who desires that all people be saved. Everything follows from the acceptance of this call. The sanctifying work of the Holy Spirit opens us to receive grace and boldness to do the work of God. It is not only difficult but impossible to do the purpose and work of God in our own strength (Zechariah 4:6).

The apostle Peter tells us that we all are called and chosen, only to different assignments. In the beatitudes, the Lord Jesus extended his call to include the poor and downtrodden. No one is left behind. We are all called to be holy and set apart for our specific assignments that glorify God as Peter tells us;

> *To God's elect, exiles scattered throughout the provinces of Pontus, Galatia, Cappadocia, Asia, and Bithynia, who have been chosen according to the foreknowledge of God the Father, through the sanctifying work of the Spirit, to be obedient to Jesus Christ and sprinkled with his blood.*
> (1 Peter 1: 1- 2)

How do I find the purpose of God for my life? It is through the sanctifying work of the Holy Spirit. We have to grow in the things of God and lose interest in the things of the world. This growth in our relationship with God, in our faith and obedience to God, is what pleases the Lord to reveal His purpose for us. Our desires change and the desires and passions of God begin to consume us. God's desires and passions are revealed. Things that were not clear before, becomes crystal clear. This is how the prophet Isaiah described it; *"Your teachers will be hidden no more; with your own eyes you will see them. Whether you turn to the right or to the left, your ears will hear a voice behind you, saying, "This is the way; walk in it."* (Isaiah 30:20-21). Our purpose becomes tangible, and we are able to say, this is what I have to do and this is where and how I have to start.

As we delight in the Lord, He guides us and shows us what to do. Psalm 37:4 tells us to, *"Take delight in the Lord, and he will give you the desires of your heart."* As we increase our time and dedication to God and forsake the ways of the world, the Lord transforms us from inside out. Our priorities and focus change. We thus desire the things that God desires. This truth is at the heart of the revelation of the purpose of God for anyone. It is to seek God to make clear what He created us for. Seek by prayer, reading of holy books, meditation on Holy Scriptures, participation in seminars, ask godly people, carry out research etc.

The Lord has promised to answer us when we seek Him with all our heart (Matthew 7:7; Luke

11:9-10; Jeremiah 29:13-14, 33:3). One scripture tells us that no longer will someone have to teach us and tell us to know the Lord for we will all know Him from within us. In other words, the desires of God will be revealed (and known) and become plain to us. (See Hebrews 8:10-11).

Purpose Revealed Through Prayer

We often receive the purpose and call of God for our lives during (or through) prayer. Prayer is one of the ways the Lord speaks to us. During intense prayer, we come under the anointing and power of the Holy Spirit. And the Holy Spirit often reveals to us His plans and purpose at such a time. This often comes by way of speaking in other tongues. So when we fast and repent, and pray in the Spirit, in unknown tongues, the subsequent interpretation reveals the purpose and plan of God.

This is the same way Paul and Barnabas received the purpose and call of God for them. This is how it happened in Antioch as recorded in the Acts of the Apostles; *"Now in the church at Antioch there were prophets and teachers: Barnabas, Simeon called Niger, Lucius of Cyrene, Manaen (who had been brought up with Herod the tetrarch) and Saul. While they were worshiping the Lord and fasting, the Holy Spirit said, "Set apart for me Barnabas and Saul for the work to which*

I have called them." So after they had fasted and prayed, they placed their hands on them and sent them off. The two of them, sent on their way by the Holy Spirit, went down to Seleucia and sailed from there to Cyprus" (Acts 13:1-4).

This happens to this day. Thus, prayer enables us to hear what God has in mind for us.

The Marketplace Purpose Of God

Most people are called to serve God in the non-ordained purposes and stations of life. Most people refer to this as the ministry to the market-place. This does not mean that it is not a holy purpose. It is a holy call that one should receive with joy. It is an equally sacred purpose of God.

This helps us appreciate that the persons engaged in the market place and collar jobs (blue, white), and if called by the Lord to such occupations, are doing the Lord's work. They are not simply discharging their duty to their employer to earn salary or wages. They are serving God. They are sent to that office and position by God, to do His work. He keeps watch over them. Further, the Lord is aware that these are the ones that support those in the ordained calls. The apostle Paul explains the difference between the ordained offices and the call to the marketplace in his letter to the Ephesians 4:11 thus;

So Christ himself gave the apostles, the prophets, the evangelists, the pastors, and teachers, to equip his people for works of service, so that the body of Christ may be built up until we all reach unity in the faith and the knowledge of the Son of God and become mature, attaining to the whole measure of the fullness of Christ (Ephesians 4:11).

We find in the scriptures that the Lord set apart Moses, Aaron, and the Levites to perform specific tasks. Much of their work had to do with the priestly roles in the tabernacle, sacrifices, and offerings. Those Levites had no share in the inheritance of the Israelites. The Lord God was their very inheritance.

Some ordained ministers of our day have a similar call. However, the Lord directly chose and appointed several others to different non-ordained (that is to say, marketplace) purposes. These supported the work of Moses, the Levites, and the priests, as we learn in Exodus 31:2-5; *"Then the Lord said to Moses, "See, I have chosen Bezalel son of Uri, the son of Hur, of the tribe of Judah, and I have filled him with the Spirit of God, with wisdom, with understanding, with knowledge and with all kinds of skills, to make artistic designs for work in gold, silver, and bronze to cut and set stones, to work in wood, and to engage in all kinds of crafts"*

The Lord similarly called Oholiab and other workmen. The Lord also called and appointed others as worshipers, skilled soldiers, designers, and embroiderers. As in the Old Testament, the number of Levites, priests, judges, and prophets were less than the total population. During the second census of Moses (Numbers 26) the Levites were one of the least populated, the least being the descendants of Simeon. In the New Testament, the Lord Jesus appointed only twelve apostles. Using this trend it is safe to say that most people are called to serve the Lord in the marketplace. These roles complement each other. Those in the ordained roles support those in the marketplace, and vice-versa.

The kingdom of God advances when everyone accepts the unique assignment they were created for, and not seek other purposes. Thus, as an example, someone created by the Lord to serve as a nurse at the hospital ought not to seek work at the commercial bank.

Several hindrances and barriers exist in finding and accepting our marketplace purpose. When we choose an occupation based on monetary attractiveness we will lose in the end. It is better to choose an occupation where we can serve with peace and grow in it. This ought to be based on our talents, skills, and gifts we have. And as we improve our capabilities in that occupation and serve more people our reward grows as a result. Our reward improves with time, as our gifts are put to use. We need not volunteer and go and serve where we do not have the grace of God in that area.

In Luke 9 the Lord Jesus met a young man who wanted to volunteer and follow Jesus. The Lord Jesus realized that this man would not make it, and possibly his motive was not right. This helps us understand that we cannot volunteer or call ourselves to the Lord's service. In this same story, the Lord Jesus invited others and they all gave excuses. Some of these excuses related to business, financial and social gains.

> *As they were walking along the road, a man said to him, "I will follow you wherever you go." Jesus replied, "Foxes have dens and birds have nests, but the Son of Man has no place to lay his head." He said to another man, "Follow me." But he replied, "Lord, first let me go and bury my father." Jesus said to him, "Let the dead bury their dead, but you go and proclaim the kingdom of God." Still, another said, "I will follow you, Lord; but first let me go back and say goodbye to my family." Jesus replied, "No one who puts a hand to the plow and looks back is fit for service in the kingdom of God"* (Luke 9:57-62).

Farther down the road, in Luke 18 another rich young ruler shows up. He seemed to be an honest and sincere man with a very important request. He must have spent sleepless nights pondering how to get to heaven. He wanted to know what to do to enter the kingdom of heaven. He satisfied Jesus except for one thing, his wealth. The Lord Jesus told him to go sell all his possessions, give the money to the poor, and then come and follow him. Scripture tells us that, at the mention of sales of his wealth, he walked away sad, because he had a lot of it.

The Lord Jesus told the apostles that *"it is easier for a camel to go through the eye of a needle than for a rich man to enter the kingdom of God"* (Luke 18:25). However, he also told them that those who left their earthly wealth, to pursue the kingdom will be heavily rewarded. They will receive true riches many times over in this world and in the world to come, eternal life.

Financial and social considerations are a hindrance to accepting the purpose of God. Foremost on our minds are questions related to money. How shall I survive in such a service? How much do they pay? How will others view me in such an occupation? However, the Lord Jesus made it clear that those who accepted and followed their purposes need not worry about finances. Here is the assurance of the Lord Jesus; *"Truly I tell you," Jesus replied, "no one who has left home or brothers or sisters or mother or father or children or fields for me and the gospel will fail to receive a hundred times as much in this present age: homes, brothers, sisters, mothers, children, and fields—along with persecutions—and in the age to come eternal life"* (Mark 10:29-30).

The Lord assures anyone who diligently pursues the purpose of God for their lives that they will receive a hundredfold return in this present age, and in the after here, eternal life. Following God is worth it. This truth emboldens us to seek, find and do the purpose of God for our lives. The Lord is not against wealth, except the mammon type of wealth, as we discern from these. One does not have to focus on wealth but look for an avenue to serve God and His people, and use any wealth that the Lord sends our way to bless God, self, and others in that order.

The wealth we have belongs to God (see Psalm 150:10, and Haggai 2:8, James 1:17). *"Every good and perfect gift is from above, coming down from the Father of the heavenly lights, who does not change like shifting shadows Every good and perfect gift comes from God"* (James 1:17). We are stewards of the gifts and graces of God (see Luke 16). We have to use the wealth and resources at our disposal for supporting the work of God, and for food, and investments, and other good works. Paul the apostle teaches us in 2 Corinthians this important principle;

> *Now he who supplies seed to the sower and bread for food will also supply and in-*

crease your store of seed and will enlarge the harvest of your righteousness. You will be enriched in every way so that you can be generous on every occasion, and through us, your generosity will result in thanksgiving to God. This service that you perform is not only supplying the needs of the Lord's people but is also overflowing in many expressions of thanks to God. Because of the service by which you have proved yourselves, others will praise God for the obedience that accompanies your confession of the gospel of Christ, and for your generosity in sharing with them and with everyone else (2 Corinthians 9:10-13).

Not only should we give to the work of God, but we ought to save, invest, grow our finances and use what is left frugally. In this way, we are good stewards of what God has given us.

Wealth is not accumulated instantly but is built over time. As in the parable of the talents, what one has depends on the purpose and assignments the Lord has for them. We all have a certain measure of wealth. Wealth is what God uses to confirm and keep the covenant He made with our forefathers. In the book of Deuteronomy, the Lord God decreed that when we walk in diligent obedience to his will and purpose he will give us the ability and power to make wealth. This He says is to confirm, keep, and establish the covenant he swore to our forefathers.

He further promises to bless all works of our hands. *"But remember the Lord your God, for it is he who gives you the ability to produce wealth, and so confirms his covenant, which he swore to your ancestors, as it is today"* (Deuteronomy 8:18), and to enable us abound in good works (2 Corinthians 9:11), and our generosity will lead to thanksgiving to God.

When we do not have any certain source of wealth, we have to seek the Lord to show us what to do to serve Him. As we see in the book of the prophet Habakkuk, we have to stand at our prayer guard posts and ask the Lord for a vision, plan, creativity, idea, or a concept we can use to receive wealth from Him. The prophet Habakkuk said, *"I will stand at my watch, and station myself on the ramparts; I will look to see what he will say to me"* (Habakkuk 2:2-4). Others may discourage you, and tell you not to ask or seek God for something like wealth.

The purpose the Lord has given us requires resources and this is what the Lord says about it; *"I will give you hidden treasures, riches stored in secret places, so that you may know that I am the LORD, the God of Israel, who summons you by name"* (Isaiah 45:3). Most people who came up with great inventions, creativity, breakthrough innovations, had some supernatural breakthrough at some point.

For the Lord to bless the work of your hands requires you to put your hands to something. You must be involved in some gainful activity. You have to put your hands on the plow and never look back (Luke 9:62), and do something that advances the kingdom, blesses God and His people. The Lord uses this to bless you too.

This point is important because most folks may fear to seek and do the purpose of God because they think they would not be able to survive financially. The Lord has already made provisions for those engaged in His work. This provision is not very far from you. It is in your hands. What is in your hands? There is something that you already have, and the Lord wants to reveal to you as soon as you seek and enter His service. Remember that we are not to steal, beg or cheat.

We are commanded to work diligently and to live a frugal life as in this counsel in the book of Proverbs. *"Go to the ant, you sluggard; consider its ways and be wise! It has no commander, no overseer or ruler, yet it stores its provisions in summer, and gathers its food at harvest. How long will you lie there, you sluggard? When will you get up from your sleep? A little sleep, a little slumber, a little folding of the hands to rest— and poverty will come on you like a thief and scarcity like an armed man"* (Proverbs 6:6-11).

Given that we expose ourselves to failure if

we work outside the purpose of God, we have to ask God for what He wants us to do. Where else would we go to ask for means to keep alive and glorify God? In Luke 11 the Lord Jesus teaches us at length to ask. He was speaking about bread, fish, eggs and the Holy Spirit. *"So I say to you: Ask and it will be given to you; seek and you will find; knock and the door will be opened to you. For everyone who asks receives; the one who seeks finds; and to the one who knocks, the door will be opened. Which of you fathers, if your son asks for a fish, will give him a snake instead? Or if he asks for an egg, will give him a scorpion? If you then, though you are evil, know how to give good gifts to your children, how much more will your Father in heaven give the Holy Spirit to those who ask him!"* (Luke 11: 9-13).

Our only caveat in this matter is that we should ask with the desire and attitude to please God. We should not ask God to send us wealth to use for purposes of greed, self-aggrandizing or some sinful purpose. Our attitude should be to receive wealth from God and become a channel to use it for the advancement of his kingdom, to bless Him, ourselves and others.

The tangible wealth should not come before the true wealth. True wealth includes our love of God and people, faith, hope, joy, peace, patience, kindness, and such fruit of the Spirit. If we ask according to His will he hears us (1 John 5:14).

We have not because we ask not, or ask for wrong motives. *"You do not have because you do not ask God. When you ask, you do not receive, because you ask with wrong motives, that you may spend what you get on your pleasures"* (James 4:2-3).

It is His will to grant us a certain type and a certain amount of wealth, depending on our level of stewardship, and what we hope to use it for, as in Matthew 25. When we do not steward His wealth, gifts and talents appropriately even the little we have is to be taken away from us, and given to someone actively involved in doing the Lord's work. We have to manage any wealth, diligently on behalf of its true owner, God. In this way, the wealth we receive from Him does not ensnare him. And the wealth should not become mammon and ensnare us. It should not come first and become our focus.

Our focus should be on the Lord's assignment and purpose. If managing this wealth takes all our time and efforts, and we have no time to focus on God, then we want to come out of it. We also realize that there are several attachments and allurements in this life to take note of. In the above, cases family, wealth, business, wrong motive hindered their call. As, for them, these may hinder us from accepting the purpose and call of God for our lives. We are better off if we do not let these hinder the purpose and call the Lord has for us.

We should not focus on wealth, but seek where to serve God, and as a result, the Lord shows us what to do to receive from Him wealth of a certain type and value. God and His kingdom's priorities should come first.

Where are you called to serve? Are you in the purpose of God for your life right now? What is the purpose of God for your life? What trade or occupation are you called to? These are very important questions and not to be answered in haste or lightly. You have to diligently seek God to show you His purpose for your life. Your victory and fulfillment depend on it.

Chapter 9

Our Gifts – What Do You Have In Your Hands?

The Lord has endowed us with various gifts, skills, talents, flair, aptitude, and abilities. When we consistently use these we develop expertise, experience, and competences. Some have a greater measure of a certain gift and ability than others. All this is good and we ought to use them for the work of God. We should not wait any longer but start somewhere.

The Lord has endowed us with distinct supernatural spiritual gifts and graces too. These gifts of the Holy Spirit are the supernatural graces given to us to help us carry out the purpose of God for our lives. They are the extraordinary ability, power, and skills freely given to us. The Holy Spirit endows us with these gifts to advance, build-up, encourage, instruct, exhort, console, and comfort the body of believers.

They are also given for our personal sanctification. For some, the gift is so distinct that no one can fail to recognize that we have them. These manifest as some supernatural ability, flair, and capability. Some of these gifts are rare and special, while others are common. We ought not to boast about our spiritual gifts or any other graces we have. This is because they are freely given to us by God. We simply found out that we had them.

They are not solely for our benefit. They are given to us to advance the work of God. They are neither for sale nor commercial profit. They are tools, and when used together with those of others, produce amazing results. We are to use these supernatural gifts at the discretion, and direction of God.

What Gifts Do You Have?

The Lord created us with distinct gifts to serve Him. However, only one (or two) of these gifts will be dominant. We have to realize that we have all of the gifts of the Holy Spirit. We have all these gifts because the giver, (the Holy Spirit) lives inside of us. We should expect the gifts that are not dominant to show up from time to time. Why do we not see many gifts manifest? We have to compare this to the mechanic and the carpenter. It is for the same reason the mechanic and the carpenter rarely bring out specialized tools until there is a unique requirement for them. The gifts that are readily available or manifesting should be put to use.

In the book of Exodus, the Lord appeared to Moses in the burning bush. The Lord appointed Moses and gave him power and authority, which could not be seen by the naked eyes. Moses had this power and authority in him. He was required to use them to lead the children of Israel to the Promised Land. Moses informed the Lord that he was not the right person for that task and gave some excuses.

To help remove Moses' fear and doubt the Lord showed him how these supernatural graces and power work. Then the Lord said to him, *"What is that in your hand?" "A staff," he replied. The Lord said, "Throw it on the ground." Moses threw it on the ground and it became a snake, and he ran from it. Then the Lord said to him, "Reach out your hand and take it by the tail." So Moses reached out and took hold of the snake and it turned back into a staff in his hand. "This," said the Lord, "is so that they may believe that the Lord, the God of their fathers—the God of Abraham, the God of Isaac and the God of Jacob—has appeared to you"* (Exodus 4: 2-5).

God equipped an ordinary person, a shepherd, into a new Moses with power and authority from God. And miraculous signs and wonders started following Moses. We have to rely on the

Lord to use us in the purpose He has given us.

We have in us the gifts to use to do the will of God. The widow at Zarephath and the widow with olive oil had something useful the Lord put in their hands. They had something to start with. The prophets Elijah and Elisha multiplied what the widows already had. They had something to begin with. In case of prophet Elijah's, the widow at Zarephath had; water, a handful of flour in a jar and a "little oil" (1 Kings 17:12).

While for the prophet Elisha the widow with oil had, "a little oil". However, this is not how the widow described it. She believed she had nothing, she told the prophet she had nothing, except a small jar of olive oil. Elisha asked her; *"How can I help you? Tell me, what do you have in your house?", "Your servant has nothing there at all,"* she said, *"except a small jar of olive oil." Elisha said, "Go around and ask all your neighbors for empty jars. Don't ask for just a few. Then go inside and shut the door behind you and your sons. Pour oil into all the jars, and as each is filled, put it to one side."* (2 Kings 4:2-4).

Whatever little they had was multiplied by God many times over. We too stand the risk of limiting God, by exclaiming, I am nothing, I have nothing. What can I do?

We need not fear to use our gifts, talents, skills, abilities, and expertise to do God's work. When we constantly use these gifts they grow and strengthen. Yet our gifts and talents often only point to our life's purpose and call. Other times they place us right in the center of the purpose of God for our lives. They are a useful starting point for us to move into the mission the Lord has for us.

The apostle Peter and his brother Andrew were skilled fishermen. The Lord Jesus called them, *"Come follow me", Jesus said, "and I will make you fishers of men"* (Mark 1:17). They had great fishing skills, abilities, and expertise. They would henceforth use these abilities to build the kingdom of God. Similarly, scripture tells us that the apostle Paul grew in the use of his various gifts (Act 13:1). When we do not use these gifts they remain dormant.

The Revelation Of Gifts And Graces Of God

Gifts and purposes can be revealed by prophecy. Other times gifts reveal themselves and manifest without any prompt. When we realize that we have a spiritual gift, it is advisable for us to place ourselves in the service or support of others more experienced in the use of the gift we have received.

We further, need to do our best to increase our knowledge, wisdom, and understanding and use and operation of this gift. For the gifts received through prophecies, we need to test whether the prophecies are genuine. This is very scriptural as in (1 John 4:1). *"Dear friends, do not believe every spirit, but test the spirits to see whether they are from God because many false prophets have gone out into the world"*. What any prophet tells us should line up with the character, nature, and word of God. It is much better if the prophecy confirms what we already received earlier from another valid source. The Bereans examined what the apostle Paul taught them to ensure that the teachings lined up with the scriptures. *"Now the Berean Jews were of more noble character than the Thessalonians, for they received the message with eagerness and examined the Scriptures every day to see if what Paul told them was true"* (Acts 17:11).

We encourage everyone to honor and support any genuine prophet. Scripture, however, warns us that in the last days many false prophets shall arise. They will deceive people including if possible the elect (Matthew 7:15; 24:11,24; 2 Peter 2:1).

Another way to give credence to what we receive from any prophet is to verify the track record of the prophet. This means that what the prophet prophesied in the past must have come to pass. Good prophets have a badge of suffering and are known to suffer much throughout their lives (James 5:10; Acts 7:52; Matthew 5:12; Luke 6:23).

What about the open and secret life of such

a prophet and the fruit in the life of the prophet? Whereas, we all fail, we ought to be careful when we come across a prophet who does not wish to repent. Anyone speaking forth the word of God is worth giving attention to. Whereas, we are not all called to the office of the prophet, we are required to evangelize, to witness. We have to speak forth the truth of God's word to encourage, comfort and build up others. When we do this it carries a similar weight and is part of prophecy, given that these words can edify and comfort a person. In some instances, the Holy Spirit enables us to prophesy even though we are not prophets.

Prophetic utterances are not limited to prophets as we learn in Luke 2. A devout and righteous man living in Jerusalem called Simeon prophesied over the little child Jesus. "Then Simeon blessed them and said to Mary, his mother: *"This child is destined to cause the falling and rising of many in Israel, and to be a sign that will be spoken against, so that the thoughts of many hearts will be revealed. And a sword will pierce your own soul too"* (Luke 2: 34-35).

Anyone can prophesy as and when the Holy Spirit allows them. And if anyone prophesies doom or death over us we ought to speak back and reject and nullify the words. We have to emphatically and politely tell them that what they spoke will not happen to us, in the Name of Jesus. We do not have to wait until they are gone.

What if we realize this after they have left? We still have the authority Christ gave us, and we have to use it to speak and nullify whatever wrong words they spoke over us. We do not have to accept such prophecies as they are contrary to the nature of God. Our response should be swift and the same, even though the words are not spoken over us by a prophet. We live under grace, and the Lord accepts us back when we repent (Luke 15: 11-32; Ezekiel 18; Mark 1:15; Matthew 18:22). We have to honor and respect the prophets because they support, build and comfort us. There are genuine prophets out there. And the Lord still appoints and calls various other people to the office of prophets.

Several Scriptures help us know the nature and operation of gifts. The book of Romans 12 has a list of them, including that of prophecy, serving, teaching, exhortation, giving and leadership. While Ephesians 4:11 elaborates the calls to specific offices. These offices are that of the apostle, prophet, evangelist, pastor, and teacher. In the entire chapters of 1 Corinthians 12; 13; and 14 Paul teaches about gifts. Paul helps us to understand how to use our gifts to serve the body of Christ.

Some of the gifts include the ones in Ephesians and Romans. The various gifts are often categorized as; the power gifts (the gift of faith, the gift of healing, and the gift of miracles). While the revelatory gifts include; the gifts of the word of wisdom, word of knowledge, and the gift of discernment of spirits). Further, there are the vocal or speaking gifts. They include the gift of speaking in tongues, interpretation of tongues and the gift of prophecy. Several other gifts do not fall into the above categories. Some few include; the gifts of service; exhortation; generosity; leading; mercy, visions; helps and administration.

Other extraordinary graces and gifts are to be found in several places in the bible. For example, God appointed and equipped craftsmen with extra-ordinary skills to build the temple. They were to equip and teach others those skills (Exodus 35:30-32, Isaiah 11). As a result of such a combination of gifts, they accomplished elaborate feats and tasks never done or seen before. We learn from other Scriptures that the Lord gave graces to others for praise, worship, and music. King David chose musician, and Jehoshaphat did the same.

King Jehoshaphat chose some people to sing and praise the Lord during battle. These led with worship and singing during the battle to rout out the Moabites and the Ammonites as described in 2 Chronicles 20:21; *"After consulting the people, Jehoshaphat appointed men to sing to the Lord and to praise Him for the splendor of his holiness as they went out at the head of the army, saying: "Give thanks to the Lord, for his love endures forever."* This resulted in the total defeat of the enemies of Israel at that battle, by the Lord

God. Jehoshaphat did not have to engage in any fight.

The Holy Spirit has limitless graces and gifts. These are available to them that yield to receive them. We have to use these gifts with humility and in Christian love, even when we have to use them to correct someone. This is because of the extraordinary and unconditional love of God for all of us. Further, it is because most people fall into trouble, due to partial to no fault of their own. They can be won back if reached out in love.

Fan Into Flame The Gifts You Have

What extraordinary gifts or supernatural graces do you have? Those whose gifts have sprung forth should use them without any apology and with praise and gratitude to God. And those who think that they do not have any gift need to know that they do have them. They need to ask and seek God for a revelation and activation of their gifts. The apostle Paul exhorts Timothy, his spiritual son, to fan into flame the gift he received and is in him when hands were laid on him (2 Timothy 1:6). These gifts help us move into the purpose of God for our lives. They are a toolbox handy to use as the occasion requires. They may or may not be the same as our purpose.

Chapter 10

Overlooked Purpose And Call Of God

You may still be unclear as to what the purpose of God for you is. You may say, "I still do not know the purpose, or mission, or plan or assignment of God for my life". What do I have to do? This is a genuine concern, and you should continually ponder it. Perhaps you have sensed that the Lord created you for some specific purpose? And there is a meaning of your life? Do not stop until you find the purpose of God for our life.

You need to desire with all your heart to know with absolute assurance why the Lord created you, what His purpose for you on earth is. And stop at nothing short of that. You do not have to judge yourself or anybody. Paul did not judge anyone. Instead, he stated in his letter to the Philippians his firm resolve. This is how he framed it; *"But one thing I do: Forgetting what is behind and straining toward what is ahead, I press on toward the goal to win the prize for which God has called me heavenward in Christ Jesus"* (Philippians 3: 13-14).

Your Purpose Is Unique

God is not limited to the marketplace or the ordained examples above. It may be that the Lord has called you to look after orphans or widows or strangers. His wish could be that you support a few of them or thousands of them. That too He will make clear once you set your hands on the plow (start work). The desire and burden to do this work, will consume you most of the time. You will find no peace doing something else. And the Lord will confirm your assignment by sending in supernatural help for your assignment to move on.

The Lord would confirm it by making the resources available despite the challenges you may encounter. The other comfort would be the willingness and enthusiasm of others to support you. This should give you the sign that you are most likely in the perfect purpose of God for your life. This type of work equally glorifies the Lord and enables those less fortunate to have a chance in life. You are possibly called to intercede for the various causes and persons, known and unknown.

You are possibly called to intercede for the

conversion of people in your locality. So the Lord places in your heart the desire and burden to intercede. And after several years to your knowledge, possibly not a single person is converted. Only after a long while will you witness changes as a result of your effort. And as they begin to turn to the Lord, your community is revived. Perhaps, you will witness no noticeable changes in your lifetime, and hardly anyone will notice you. Such is the purpose of God for your life.

You are possibly called to generosity, to support financially those involved in the work of God. This happens when the Lord has provided you the means. In Mark 9:41, the Lord Jesus said that *"Truly I tell you, anyone who gives you a cup of water in my name because you belong to the Messiah will certainly not lose their reward"*. And so Gaius was commended by the apostle John (see 3 John 1-9) for his hospitality compared to Diotrephes who refused to support and provide hospitality to the missionaries. The Lord's vineyard is so vast that he can place you in a service you least expect to be significant.

The Meaning Of Life

You may still be unclear as to what the purpose of God for you is. Do not stop until you find the purpose of God for your life. What is the meaning of life? The meaning of life and the reason for our existence baffles or puzzles many people. Why are we here on earth? Many people openly ask, or ponder. And rightly so given the many challenges we face. The meaning of life becomes easier to comprehend when we find and do what the Lord created us for. At whatever age, it is not late to fulfill the purpose God created us for.

We may not be able to complete it in our lifetime and the Lord will look for others to continue where we stopped. That is what happened to Moses and others. Moses handed over to Joshua. We need to appreciate the importance of our existence in the perspective of God, not ours. When we swerve to the wrong route, we need to make a comeback.

Mark Twain an Englishman, once said that there are two most important days of our lives. The first one according to him; is the day we were born, and the second most important day of our lives is the day we find out why. In his wisdom, there is a special reason and purpose for our birth and most importantly we need to find out why.

We already know it in part. The chief end of all human beings is to glorify God; that is to know, love, praise, worship, serve and enjoy God and live with Him eternally. We are here on earth to glorify Him. We came to the world as His work of art. We are created by a potter for a certain purpose, shaping it as seemed best to Him (Jeremiah 18:4b). We had no choice or voice in our creation. We never had any input or discussion as to what our gender, color, height, weight, should be. We also did not choose our geographical location, date, time and year of birth or domicile. We were born with a set of characteristics and innate gifts, skills and abilities all without our input. We never sought our parents even though they love and care for us.

The potter determined all these for us. Since God, the potter, is perfect, we are therefore the right fit for a specific purpose of His. We are in the right place at the right time. The book of Esther inspires us to believe and say with confidence that we are made for such a time as this (Esther 4:14). It is fair to conclude that only God knows why He created us, (that is, our purpose) and is pleased to reveal it to us.

We have freedom of choice. However, it is better to cooperate with the Lord and follow the leading of the Holy Spirit, and yield this freedom over to Him. The apostle Paul tells us in his letter to the Romans that we will never fail (we are more than conquerors) when we live a life controlled by the Holy Spirit. He says *"For those who are led by the Spirit of God are the children of God"* (Romans 8:14). And he goes on to say that the Holy Spirit helps us when we yield to Him.

When we forgo, yield and surrender our ambitions to that of God, we will find the purpose of God and do it. The Lord Jesus had to forgo his free-will and self-will to do the will of the Father

(John 5:19, 20, 30, Luke 22:42). We ought to run the race marked out for us. The letter to the Hebrews 12:1-2 reminds us that there is a race the Lord has marked out for us; *"Therefore, since we are surrounded by such a great cloud of witnesses, let us throw off everything that hinders and the sin that so easily entangles. And let us run with perseverance the race marked out for us, fixing our eyes on Jesus, the pioneer, and perfecter of faith"*. We note that the cloud of witnesses and heroes of the Bible triumphantly completed their races.

God knows best what we ought to do. This truth may look strange, and yet we experience it to some extent in several organizations. This is similar to what happens in the military and companies worldwide. The commanders, managers, and superiors have the last say on what the subordinates, staff, employees should do. They base decisions on the vision and mission of the organization, and their judgments and interests. There is little choice for those under them to go against the decision of the organization.

As we already know, obedience to these superiors is key to retaining your place in such organizations. Misbehavior, defiance, and deviation from the vision of such organizations often lead to loss of favor or disagreement. And all these happen through an established channel of communication. And we too need to learn to hear and obey what God is telling us. We have a mighty and loving God, who is ready to reccive us back. And we are blessed to know that He has our best interests at heart, and promised not to place us where we are not able. We need not worry about the minute details ahead of us. As we learn to hear his voice, the Lord speaks to us what He wants us to do.

We Ought To Be Certain

Many Christians do not know for certain if they are living in the purpose of God for their lives. Most are not certain as to whether the occupation, job, assignment, and engagement they are involved in, is what God created them for. There are others with some level of awareness without clarity. A few others are not aware not because of their fault.

The apostle Paul encountered a similar scenario. In the book of the Acts of the Apostles Paul asked some disciples (Christians) he found in Ephesus if they had received the Holy Spirit. Their answer stunned Paul. They told Paul that they had never even heard that there was such a thing as the Holy Spirit (Acts 19:2). Most Christians have not heard that there is such a thing as the specific purpose of God for each one of them.

Only a few imagine they have a specific mission, assignment, of God for their lives.

The Purpose And Call Of God Is For All

While others believe that the purpose, plan, and call of God must be for a special group. They believe that such a beautiful purpose must be for the pastors, priests, prophets, evangelists, apostles and similar servants of God as in Ephesians 4:11.

We oftentimes stretch our imagination further to include in this group other blessed Christians working in harsh environments or those with mystical calls. Others believe that those that undertake risky missions to win pagans are included. We then add to the list, those social volunteer workers in tight locations of the world and those trapped in hostile places. We include the medical volunteers and the like.

We are blessed that we can seek, know and do the purpose of God for our lives. And thus co-labor with God in His mission for us. We need not be afraid anymore. Besides, it is the only sure way for us to live a life of peace, joy, and fruitfulness. The purpose of God is the place where the Lord God guarantees us His protection, safety, and provision. We no longer have to struggle and hustle unnecessarily away from what the Lord has called us to do. We have to face challenges in the arena the Lord has created us for.

The good news is that all alive on earth today have a divine purpose and destiny. The most ordinary Christian has a call on his life. The greatest alive has this divine destiny. The non-Christian has a purpose. The pagan is called. Our neighbors are called. No one is too young or too old to receive and do the purpose of God for their lives, and as an example, Moses was called to lead the children of Israel from Egypt to the Promised Land when he was 80 years of age.

Learn To Hear The Voice Of God

As happened to Moses, we need humility, reverence, and sensitivity to hear the voice of God. Moses heard God consistently and obeyed God faithfully. There is no doubt that Moses achieved victory in his purpose and assignment because he heard and obeyed God consistently. There is, therefore, an urgent need to learn to hear the voice of God. Once we learn to hear and recognize the voice of God it is easier to fulfill the mission the Lord created us for. We can grow in this.

God is always speaking; His mighty station broadcasts continually. God speaks day and night even when we are asleep. He reaches us better, in most cases, when we are asleep. He is always broadcasting. Why then, are we not able to hear the voice of God? The answer is both ways. Yes and No. We most times hear the voice of God, but fail to recognize it. This is where we need to learn.

The challenge is on our side, not His. God has made it fool-proof that His communication must reach us. If we fail to receive it in one way, He will find an alternative way to reach us, until we perhaps ignore all of them. God speaks to us primarily through His Word.

The Lord has already spoken the greatest portion of His heart, mind, wish and desires to, counsel us, comfort us, correct us or bless us (see Hebrews 1:3). What the Lord God, His prophets, and the Lord Jesus His son, spoke already is freely available. Further, His apostles, prophets, priests, servants, evangelists, are all around us, and continue to speak the heart, mind and truth of God day and night. In one of the parables the Lord Jesus gave in Luke, the Lord told the rich man; *"If they do not listen to Moses and the Prophets, they will not be convinced even if someone rises from the dead"* (Luke 16:31).

Given that the voice of God is all around us we require humility, reverence, and sensitivity to make it out from all the chaos and noise surrounding us. We ought to read the Bible and other inspired books prayerfully, and that makes a huge difference. Suppose, we read the Bible as any other novel or as any other secular book, then it won't speak to us. It will remain silent, even when we read obvious passages. We ought to receive revelation and inspiration as we read those inspired books. The words in the Bible should tell us what to do, regarding a particular situation we are currently facing. This comes through prayerful meditation leading to revelation. We ought to meditate and seek revelation out of it, as much of it is in metaphors, similes, parables, and hidden meaning.

When we have adequate revelation from the Word of God, then the nature of God, the likes and dislikes of God, the wisdom and counsel of God are known to us. We will know the heart of God in any given situation. Should I take this job or not, should I marry this lady or the other, which city should I move to? Our decisions are taken in this context of the will, nature, and heart of God. We will find it easy and simple to make decisions.

Further, God speaks to us through dreams and visions. We all dream. While the sciences give us more proof of this. God has spoken through dreams and visions for thousands of years to His children. Those that pay attention and have learned to hear this way, benefit greatly. God also warns us in dreams about what our enemies plan to do to us, long before these enemies complete their plans. We have ample time to heed the warning and frustrate their plans.

When we sleep we go through various stages of altered consciousness. We become drowsy, and fall into initially light sleep. We end up in deep sleep. From deep sleep we retrace, this path to light sleep and wakefulness. Most people believe that we have vivid dreams in between the deep sleep and light sleep. However, they believe that we also experience dreams during all the other stages of sleep. The phase of vivid dreaming is termed as the Rapid Eye Movement phase of sleep. As the name suggests, our eyes move rapidly to and fro while we dream at this stage. We are able to remember most dreams during this phase, and that may be why most initially believed it was the only dream phase during sleep.

The Lord counsels us at night in our dreams. He gives us sensitive details and secrets about ourselves, others, or things, details we would never find anywhere else. The Lord also reveals to us who we are (our true selves) in dreams. This is because we are not exactly whom we claim to be, when we are awake. God is able to dissect this and help us know our weak areas.

As soon as we wake up, we need to write any of these dreams down and pray to God to interpret and reveal to us what each dream means. As we grow in our Christian faith, the meaning of dreams and interpretation becomes plain to us. We are able to use what the Lord tells us in dreams to live in victory. As for any language, the dream language is learned and perfected with practice, and thus takes time.

There are many other ways the Lord speaks to us including; events and circumstances, His servants (prophets, preachers, evangelists), creation, nature and those near us. God speaks through prayer, godly counsel, nature, the people around us, thoughts, visions and many other ways. We need not despair because once we set our hearts on God He will find some way to reach us.

It is so encouraging to know for sure that the Lord has spoken to us to accomplish something. We receive faith, courage, strength, and boldness to do it. It becomes impossible for anyone to confuse, blackmail or deceive us, knowing we have heard from God.

The heroes of the bible succeeded because they heard God and obeyed. These include Moses, Joshua, David, Paul, Peter and many others. As a result of recognizing what the Lord has spoken, we will no longer be afraid or anxious. The prophets who heard from God recorded what they heard. And what they recorded is happening all around us to this hour. We ought to record what the Lord tells us, and track to see how they play out and are fulfilled. We ought to start by obeying what the Lord has already spoken, and that opens the way for Him to speak more to us.

Chapter 11

Obey What God Tells You

Satan resists God's purposes and plans for us. He tries his best to ensure that we do not come to know and do the purpose the Lord created us for. We thus, have to beware and make every effort to resist him. The main way to know the will, purpose and plan of God for our lives is to seek it from the Lord God Himself. This requires prayer and extensive meditation on the word of God, the Holy Scriptures.

This point cannot be emphasized enough. The word and spirit must agree. It is written in the prophet Jeremiah thus; *"For I know the plans I have for you," declares the Lord, "plans to prosper you and not to harm you, plans to give you hope and a future. Then you will call on me and come and pray to me, and I will listen to you. You will seek me and find me when you seek me with all your heart. I will be found by you"* (Jeremiah 29:11-14).

The Lord knows the purpose He created us for. And how can we find it? The answer is when we seek Him with all our hearts. In summary, the Lord reveals His purpose for our lives when we seek Him with all our hearts. That settles the matter. We have to seek for as long as it takes. We need to receive confirmation(s) to give us confidence that we are in the right purpose of God for our lives. We have to be filled with peace. This is the type of peace that Paul describes as "the peace that surpasses understanding."

We have to learn how to hear God's voice. This means we need to know and recognize the various ways the Lord communicates to us his children. We have to be sensitive, reverent, and humble to receive the voice of God. This is because God has to communicate His purpose, and plans to us in some way. How to hear the voice of God can be learned over time. We are better able to hear the voice of the Lord when we determine to grow in our relationship with Him. We have to expect and know that the Lord is always communicating with us. The challenge is on our side. We are not able to receive due to the many noise and chaos around us.

The Lord speaks continually all year round. The Lord speaks even while we are asleep. The noise around us drowns the signals of the voice of God to us. How do we get rid of this noise? We have to learn to hear all the time. How do we tune-in correctly and all the time? That is what we have to learn.

We have to recognize the Holy Spirit's presence in situations. When we recognize the Holy Spirit presence in situations, we are able to make out the voice of God from other voices. When we do not, we risk missing his voice and dismissing it as one of the noises of no consequence. The prophet Elijah realized this. He knew and sensed it in his spirit.

The Lord may send various people to us to alert us of many important things He wants us to pay attention to, and this key helps us not to dismiss them. We will not think that these have come to trouble our well-earned peace or trespass our space. For the most critical messages, the Lord always finds a way to repeatedly bring them to our attention. He does it several times. Except that we may miss it, if at that time we are taken up by pride, and are not sensitive enough or reverent enough. For example, a man in shabby clothes may alert us that there is danger ahead and the bridge is broken. Without sensitivity, humility, and reverence, we may easily dismiss such a person and plunge in a flood plain or river downstream.

Hear And Recognize God's Voice

Since the Old Testament times, we are all commanded to hear and obey the voice of God. Sometimes we find a double or triple emphasis placed on hearing, listening, hearkening to the voice of God. We are required to hear, hear-diligently, or hearken-diligently. The voice of God is of tremendous importance. God's greatest concern through-out the years, has always been the same. His concern is that we do not hear, we do not heed, we do not pay attention, we do not diligently hear, we do not obey His voice. A lot is tied to it, such as health, and progress. To diligently hear and obey the voice of God means the difference between life and death, health and prosperity.

This truth still stands since God remains the same. Moses could not move an inch or do anything without hearing the voice of God. This secured for them water and food and defeat of all enemies. The Kings could not go to war at all before getting clearance from God. The Lord Jesus said the same thing in Matthew 7:24. *"Therefore everyone who hears these words of mine and puts them into practice is like a wise man who built his house on the rock."* Yet we cannot obey what we have not heard. To hear, we have to be tuned in, and correctly. To tune-in correctly requires being close to the receiver, or broadcast set.

Thus, we need to be close to the Holy Spirit, to hear the voice of God correctly. We have to be the sheep that follow the shepherd. In John 10:27 the Lord Jesus revealed to us the simplicity and key to hearing the voice of God. This is what He said, "My sheep listen to my voice; I know them, and they follow me". This is a heavily loaded verse. It involves, active listening, paying attention, relationship to the speaker, acquaintance with the voice, knowledge of the voice-source, and diligently doing what is said.

We should remember that God also speaks to us through circumstances. As we grow and mature spiritually our life circumstances shifts in a new direction. And that could also mean the Lord's speaking to us to take a new direction. As you notice, the transition is a steady move, and most likely not by leaps and bounds. Not all circumstances means the voice of God, and we need to discern, as for other voices.

Obey The Ordinary Everyday Voice Of God

The Lord has over the years spoken His heart out, in the Old Testament and the New Testament. He continues to do this in our days through His devoted servants. He has made known, His mind, heart, nature, likes and dislikes. There are plenty of things the Lord has already spoken that need our action and attention.

We have to act and do those things that He has already spoken to us. As the Lord Jesus said "my sheep listen to my voice".

There are certainly things we cannot find in black and white in the scriptures. For example, we cannot find in the scriptures which town or city the Lord requires us to stay in, which car to buy, which school to go to, or who to marry. Yet, scripture provides plenty of wisdom, truth, insight, foresight, knowledge that when pulled together and prayerfully woven together, answers any question troubling anyone, including where to live or whom to marry. And with the help of other godly persons and the witness of the Holy Spirit inside, and confirmation, the room for making the right decision increases, and error is narrowed.

In other instances, we do not have to go that far, except to truthfully examine our motives for the decision, and see if it pleases God and lines up with His nature and character. What would Jesus do in this situation? Does the decision I am struggling with give God the greatest glory? We may find sooner or later, that most of the decisions we are struggling with does not match to the nature and heart of God and are better shelved. And to our delight the ones that please Him are easily solved.

And for us to learn to hear the voice of God we ought to start with obedience to the already spoken voice of God. Further, we can move to the everyday clear voice of God reaching us. Also, we can ask God to show us things, teach us things or give us prompts. To hear and recognize the voice of God requires us to know the scriptures in some depth. This helps us to weed out the voices coming from the enemy.

The voice of God must line up with the Scriptures and the nature and character of God. A voice instructing us to commit a crime, a wrong, or to sin is certainly not the voice of God. This is because such a voice does not line up with the word of God and the nature of God. We can seek counsel and guidance from godly people to help us during such times. When we recognize that the Lord has spoken, we need to obey. This requires our action and no delay, but we need not rush when we are not sure.

When We Seem To Have Less Than Enough Light

Other times we may have to move ahead with less than enough word or guidance. And see what happens. We can withdraw if things begin to falter, but if we do not falter, and all is well, we simply continue. The apostle Paul seemed to have faced such a scenario. He describes how he and his companions faced danger in Asia. He said, *"We do not want you to be uninformed, brothers and sisters, about the troubles we experienced in the province of Asia. We were under great pressure, far beyond our ability to endure, so that we despaired of life itself"* (2 Corinthians 1:8). So we believe that Paul aborted this mission. He possibly moved ahead, knowing that if all went well it would be the Lord's confirmation.

When we do not have enough light to use to move on, and we are in the purpose of God, and we do not have any ill intentions or a wrong motivation, we are required to move ahead. This is exactly the advice the prophet Samuel gave King Saul. *"The Spirit of the LORD will come powerfully upon you, and you will prophesy with them; and you will be changed into a different person. Once these signs are fulfilled, do whatever your hand finds to do, for God is with you"* (1 Samuel 10:6-7). There is no need being paralyzed when the Holy Spirit has clearly granted us work to do, and seek God for more information on what next.

In the purpose of God, we have the assurance that the Lord will see us through. We have to trust that either the Lord will make things clearer along the way, or the Lord will make it hard for us to move beyond a certain red line. This should be the case where we did not hear correctly.

This scenario often happens when we seek the Lord with a heart already bent on doing something. We have decided in our hearts to go ahead whether God likes it or not! We are simply trying to force the Lord to bless what we are firmly bent on doing. We vainly hope that the Lord stamps our plans, agrees and flag us to move on.

This is what most people describe as praying with an idol in our hearts. For example, we open up a business and ask the servants of God and the people of God to come and commission it. We realize sooner than later that the Lord was not in this plan at all. This is the primary reason for the very many failed undertakings everywhere.

In the book of the prophet Jeremiah, we meet similar cases. The people were misinformed by false prophets and ended up in disobedience and disfavor with God. The Lord told the prophet, Jeremiah, that *"I did not send them"* (Jeremiah 29:8).When we pray with an idol in our heart the response we receive may not be from the Lord. In the desert, the people put the Lord to the test. He gave them their desires and leanness of soul, a wasting disease as we learn here; *"But they soon forgot what he had done and did not wait for his plan to unfold. In the desert they gave in to their craving; in the wilderness, they put God to the test. So he gave them what they asked for, but sent a wasting disease among them"* (Psalm 106:13-15).

When we pray with a yielded heart, we are open to accepting the counsel of the Lord. When we decide the response beforehand, it is difficult to receive the counsel of God with joy. In this case, the enemy takes advantage, to tell us what our itching ears want to hear. This will be different from the answer the Lord intended. Thus, we ought to seek God with a yielded and surrendered heart. We should be ready to accept a positive or negative response from the Lord. Let the Lord's will prevail over ours. We have to lay aside our wishes and plans, and accept the Lord's desires and wishes.

Our desires shift to holy desires and passions

This helps us understand that the motivational speakers that encourage us to follow our carnal passions and desires have missed it. We need to seek the Lord's passions and desires for us. Most persons that followed their worldly desires and passions ended up by the wayside. The casualty rate is way too high as seen by the number of people living in failure, lack of peace, regret and disappointment.

Going forward it is best to check with the Lord for Him to give us His purposes and plans. In the book of first Kings 19:11-13, the prophet Elijah waited to hear the voice of God in a difficult circumstance. The Lord did not appear in the powerful wind that shattered the rocks. And after that came an earthquake and then a fire, but the Lord was not in them. Finally, the Lord appeared in a gentle whisper. The still small, voice, the prompts, the quiet time thoughts, prevail as the most likely voice of God. The neighbor, friend, or relative imparting a piece of gentle advice, counsel or rebuke need not be taken lightly. Likewise, rushed decisions may haunt us. And purposes and plans based on passions and desires not checked with God may come home to roost.

Mistakes Are Inevitable And Keep Us Humble

What if we make some mistakes? The Lord is aware of that too. We would never move if we froze due to the fear of never making a mistake. Fear is not Christian, as it erodes our faith. We need to avoid mistakes, especially those we commit when we act under undue pressure, fear and lack of peace. These are "no go" indicators. We ought to move when there is peace.

The Lord knows and is aware that we will make mistakes, and when our heart is right, He will still bless us for moving despite the little light we had. We can get right back. Paul made mistakes, Moses made mistakes, and king David made mistakes. No one is immune to mistakes. When we strive for perfection, this can prevent us from making small strides that eventually build up the big picture. Some small strides and steps will be faulty.

When we veer off the correct path, we need

to ensure that we still have the correct motive and heart towards the original purpose revealed to us. Most times it is important to pray ahead of what we are about to do - and thereafter get started, even when we do not get a green light from the Lord. The Lord in most cases will show us a red light if we are on the wrong path, thus stopping us. The Lord is gracious enough to redirect us to the right path. We improve with time.

Hearing the voice of God is an important advantage that cannot be overemphasized. Moses, the Lord Jesus, the prophets and the apostles heard God all the time. In our case, we have the Holy Spirit in us, with us and upon us, and we have to rely on Him. We have to improve our relationship, and intimate knowledge (ginosko) of the Lord God our Father, the Lord Jesus our Savior and the Holy Spirit our counselor. The prophet Isaiah captures this rightly when he says that; *"the earth will be filled with the knowledge of the LORD"* (Isaiah 11:9).